# ISLAMIC AFRICA

VOLUME 5, ISSUE 1 SPRING 2014



*Northwestern University Press*
*Evanston, Illinois*

www.islamicafricajournal.org

**Scope and Mission**: *Islamic Africa* is a peer-reviewed, multidisciplinary, academic journal published by Northwestern University Press in collaboration with the Institute for the Study of Islamic Thought in Africa (ISITA), based at Northwestern University, Evanston, Illinois. The journal incorporates *Sudanic Africa,* retaining its focus on historical sources, bibliographies, and methodologies. *Islamic Africa* promotes interaction between scholars of Islam and Africa across all continents and across historical periods. The journal welcomes papers from the humanities and the social sciences on any aspect of Islam and Muslim life pertaining to Africa, or originating from the African continent.

**Communications concerning manuscripts and editorial matters** should be addressed to Prof. Scott Reese, Editor, *Islamic Africa,* Northwestern University Press, 629 Noyes Street, Evanston, IL 60208 (USA); islamicafrica@northwestern.edu. For information about submitting manuscripts, see www.islamicafricajournal.org.

**Concerning advertising and subscriptions,** address the Managing Editor, Lauren Pretnar, Northwestern University Press, 629 Noyes Street, Evanston, IL 60208 (USA); islamicafrica@northwestern.edu. Electronic subscriptions can be purchased for institutions ($125) and individuals ($75) by visiting www.islamicafricajournal .org.

 ISSN 2154-0993.

Northwestern University Press acknowledges Marianne Jankowski for the interior design and Ahmad Faris for the journal logo. The copy editor for this issue was Paul Mendelson.

# Contents

**BOOK REVIEWS**

*Islamic Africa* is a peer-reviewed, multidisciplinary, academic journal published by Northwestern University Press in collaboration with the Institute for the Study of Islamic Thought in Africa (ISITA), based at Northwestern University, Evanston. The journal incorporates *Sudanic Africa*, retaining its focus on historical sources, bibliographies, and methodologies. *Islamic Africa* promotes interaction between scholars of Islam and Africa across all continents and across historical periods. We welcome papers on any aspect of Islam and Muslim life pertaining to Africa and/or Africans from the humanities and the social sciences, especially those originating from the African continent.

# *ARTICLES*

# Localizing Fulbe Architecture

*Mark Dike DeLancey*, DEPAUL UNIVERSITY

DOI: 10.5192/21540993050101

**ABSTRACT**

*Fulbe architecture of the Adamawa Region, Cameroon, and the Fouta Djallon region, Guinea, bear many formal similarities. Fulbe in Cameroon often point to architectural form as a marker of ethnic identity. Scholars have also perceived ethnicity, as well as Islam, as central to analyzing Fulbe architecture, drawing upon a now-outdated understanding of* pulaaku, *or Fulbeness. Instead, the Fulbe should more appropriately be perceived, especially in the realm of permanent architecture, as extraordinarily adaptive. The focus on ethnicity and Islamic faith has in fact blinded scholars to the much stronger connections that can be drawn with local architectural traditions, irrespective of religion or ethnicity.*

Identifying and defining Fulbe architecture has proven a difficult task for African art historians. The Fulbe are a people commonly thought to have originated on the west coast of Africa, but who have spread widely

I am grateful to Laamiiɗo Mohammadou Hayatou Issa, the University of Ngaoundéré, and the people of Ngaoundéré for hosting me. The writing of this article was supported by a DePaul University Research Council Grant and a Visiting Scholar Appointment at Northwestern University. The final version of this work has benefited greatly from the comments of the anonymous reviewers and Dr. M. Sani Umar.

*Islamic Africa,* VOL. 5, NO. 1, 2014. ISSN 2154-0993.  www.islamicafricajournal.org

across West and Central Africa.[1] They are closely associated with the raising of cattle, and have also played a central role in the spread of Islam in sub-Saharan Africa, particularly in the last three centuries. From the west coast, the Fulbe spread east across the continent over the centuries with the principle aim of locating new pastures for their cattle. In many places, groups of Fulbe have settled and at times come to rule over their adopted lands. Such is true in the Fouta Djallon region of Guinea, which saw the foundation of an Islamic state by Fulbe in the early eighteenth century. A century later, Fulbe in northern Cameroon formed a number of substates under the ultimate authority of the Sokoto Caliphate (figure 1).

The peregrinations and cultural changes experienced by the Fulbe over these past three centuries have raised the important question for architectural historians as to what, if anything, constitutes specifically Fulbe architecture? Two major points of view have developed regarding this question that were, in both cases, at odds with the prevailing contemporaneous scholarly notions of Fulbe identity. On the one hand, late nineteenth- and early twentieth-century scholars generally emphasized the unity of Fulbe identity, while those studying Fulbe art and architecture suggested the widespread Fulbe adoption of local architectural forms from surrounding populations wherever they settled. On the other hand, since the 1980s, the field of Fulbe studies has emphasized issues of culture change and distinctions in identity, as art historians espoused an essential unity of sedentary Fulbe architecture across the diaspora that is predicated on common values of pastoralism, a former nomadic life, and Islam.

This article argues that those studying Fulbe architecture must recognize the shift in Fulbe studies from an emphasis on a unitary identity to its malleability. It is not focused primarily on the debates over identity, but rather how those debates impact the study of architecture. The example of northern Cameroon will be employed to illustrate the pitfalls of an overemphasis on notions of cultural continuity across the Fulbe diaspora, and the absolute necessity of considering architectural expression in relation to its local context. Architecture commonly designated as Fulbe in Adamawa Region, Cameroon, is first compared in formal qualities to Fulbe architecture in the Fouta Djallon region of Guinea. The argument for architectural continuity will be placed in the context of both popular Fulbe and early scholarly discourses that emphasize a common Fulbe identity.

[1] Thierno Diallo, "Origine et migration des peuls avant le XIXe siècle," *Annales de la faculté des lettres et sciences humaines* 2 (1972): 168–74.

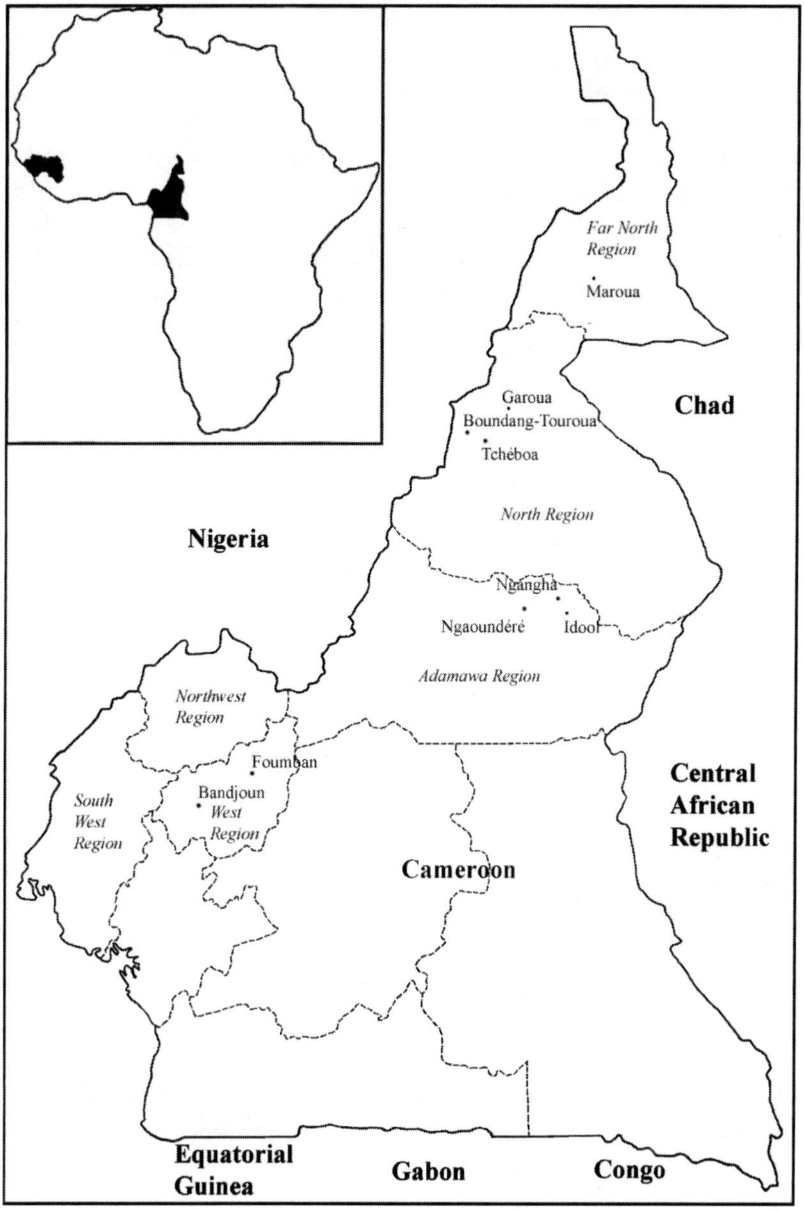


**Figure 1**
Map of Cameroon in relation to Guinea.

This orientation will be contrasted with the early literature on Fulbe architecture, which ironically focused on the acculturation of the Fulbe to their various local contexts. The shift to a more contextualized understanding of Fulbe identity formation in the 1980s provides an impetus for rejecting the notion of a specifically Fulbe architecture in Adamawa Region, Cameroon. Consideration of the architecture of neighboring ethnicities and regions will impress the distinctly local qualities of architecture built for or by Fulbe in this region, foregrounding the necessity of balancing potential ethnic or religious sources of architectural form with more immediately produced ones based on geography, climate, and political and sociocultural allegiances.

### *Fulbe Architecture in Adamawa and Fouta Djallon*

At first glance, the architecture of Adamawa Region, Cameroon, and the Fouta Djallon region, Guinea, bear many formal similarities. The strongest relationship can be drawn between elite residential and palace architecture in Adamawa and mosque architecture in Fouta Djallon. The elite architecture of Adamawa Region, and in particular of its capital Ngaoundéré, is immediately recognizable and unique in Cameroon. It is typified by a tall pointed roof topped with a small cap that reproduces the whole in miniature (figure 2). Roofs in this region, especially of elite architecture, are thatched with a particularly long, thin, and straight grass from the Adamawa plateau called *siiseeri* in Fulfulde. Thatched with cut bottom exposed, and bound at the head of the grass, the roofs possess a spectacularly smooth sloping surface. Within the palace of Ngaoundéré, the thatched roofs are all executed in this elegant manner.

This sleek surface is in contrast to most houses, which, though possessing the same basic form, have a much rougher texture to the thatching as the grasses are attached by the sturdier cut base with the tufted head exposed (figure 4). The grass stems do not snap as easily when thatching in this manner and therefore require rethatching less often. Although this method of thatching sheds rain just as effectively as the smoother method, it is not nearly as aesthetically pleasing.

Functionally speaking, the cap provides added protection for the apex of the roof, but it is not absolutely necessary (figure 5). Mimicking the whole of the roof in miniature, it participates in a tradition widespread across northern Cameroon, and surrounding regions as well, of fitting the apex of the roof with an attractive finial, whether woven of grass or crowned with pottery.

**Figure 2**

Second building (*Jawleeru Njakmukon*) in the Palace of Ngaoundéré, west façade. Ngaoundéré, Cameroon.Photo by Mark D. DeLancey, 1996.

**Figure 3**
Second building (*Jaweleeru Njakmukon*) in the Palace of Ngaoundéré, plan. Ngaoundéré, Cameroon. Drawing by Mark D. DeLancey.

The building beneath is typically constructed of courses of unbaked earth. The standard residential unit is circular in plan with the door as the only opening. Such circular plan structures may also be employed as entrances or distribution points to various quarters within a larger family compound, in which case the walls would be pierced by two or more portals. The walls are protected from sun and rain, an important consideration given the heavy rainy season on the Adamawa Plateau, by the extension of the roof to create broad eaves.

In more elaborate structures, such as in the palace of Ngaoundéré,

**Figure 4**
Binding grass thatching by the stem. Idool, Cameroon. Photo by Mark D. DeLancey, 2000.

building plans are often square or rectangular (figure 3). The walls, both exterior and interior, may be decorated with painted low relief geometric decoration. An earthen ceiling is supported from within by one or more stout earthen pillars, elements distinguishing the building type known as a *sooro*.[2] The earthen ceiling is only apparent from the interior, as are the pillars, since the thatched roof hides their existence on the exterior. The eaves extend almost to the ground, cloaking the entire building in deep shadows. The eaves are supported on wooden poles planted in a semicircular plan around each portal to create a porch. Thus the roof of what may be a square-plan building visually transforms the exterior into a subtly undulating conical form.

Elite residential architecture in the Fouta Djallon region of Guinea bears some formal similarities to that of Adamawa. As in Adamawa, residential structures are ordinarily circular in plan.[3] Wood poles may be ar-

[2] For a more in-depth look at the historical use of this building type in northern Cameroon, see Mark D. DeLancey, "The Spread of the Sooro: Symbols of Power in the Sokoto Caliphate," *Journal of the Society of Architectural Historians* 71, no. 2 (June 2012): 168–85.
[3] Jean Poujade, *Les cases décorées d'un chef du Fouta-Djiallo.* Documents d'ethnographie terrestre 1 (Paris: Gauthier-Villars, 1948).

**Figure 5**

Roof cap with framework revealed. Ngaoundéré, Cameroon. Photo by Mark D. DeLancey, 2000.

ranged in a circular fashion around the building to create a veranda. Long rafters converge above the center of the building and extend down over the walls of the building and the posts of the outer porch to create a conical form which is then thatched. Thus, the residential unit is composed of a conical thatched roof over a circular plan room (figure 6).

The walls and even the floors, beds, and other surfaces of an elite residence may be decorated with incised and painted geometric decoration. This decoration is more enveloping and of a more delicate character than the bold relief decoration usually seen on pillars and surrounding portals in Adamawa. The interior of the thatched roof, visible since there is no ceiling, may be decorated with horizontal rings of bound thatching arranged in straight or undulating lines around the interior circumference.[4]

By contrast, and in common with the entrance to the palace of Ngaoundéré, mosque architecture in the Fouta Djallon is resolutely square in plan, based on the model of the Kaʾba as encouraged by the Maliki school of Islam

[4] Ibid., 16–31; P. Creac'h, "Notes sur l'art décoratif architectural Foula du haut Fouta-Djallon," in *Comptes rendus de la première conférence internationale des africanistes de l'ouest* (Paris: Librairie d'Amérique et d'Orient Adrien-Maisonneuve, 1951), 300–312.

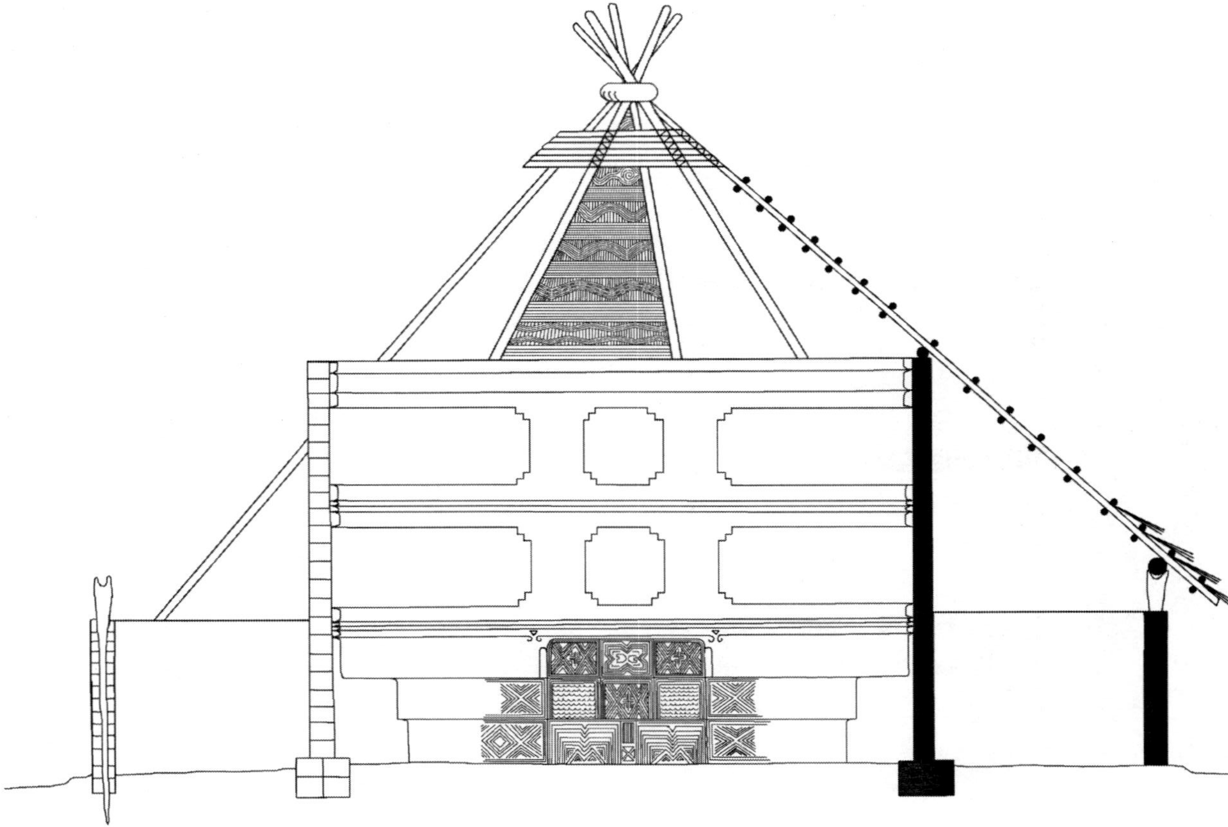

**Figure 6**

Section of a house. Dalaba, Guinea. Composite drawing by Mark D. DeLancey after Poujade, *Les Cases Décorées*, p. 8, fig. 1; p. 23, figs. 19 & 20; p. 28, fig. 31.

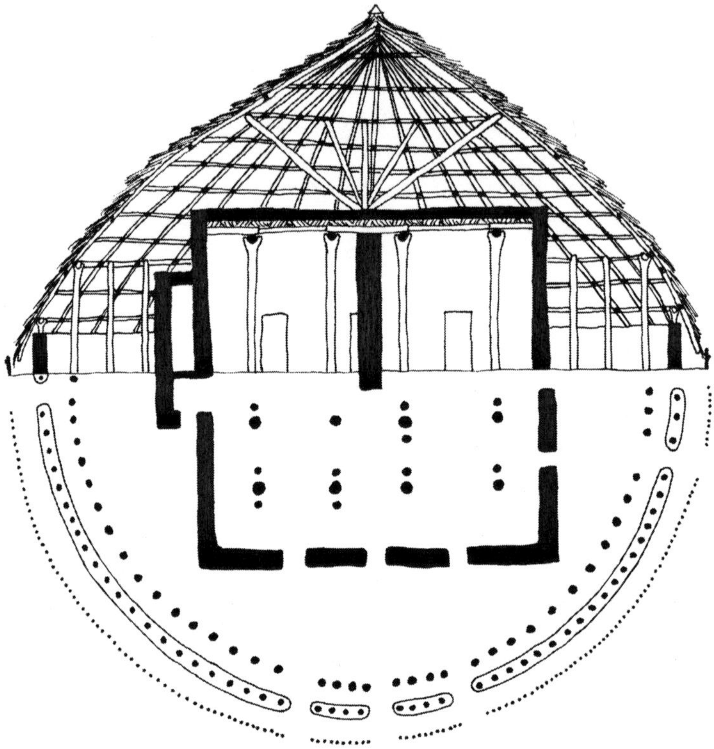

**Figure 7**
Friday Mosque of Dinguiraye, section. Plan by Mark D. DeLancey, after Prussin, *Hatumere*, p. 229, fig. 7.34b.

followed throughout West Africa.[5] The Friday Mosque of Dinguiraye, Guinea, is the largest and most spectacular example of this type (figures 7 and 8).

The plan employs triple entrances on the north, west, and south sides. A mihrab niche on the east side indicating the *qibla* completes the composition.

[5] Labelle Prussin, *Hatumere: Islamic Design in West Africa* (Berkeley: University of California Press, 1986), 184, 187. It is difficult to compare like structures in both contexts. While mosques are documented in the Fouta Djallon, these historical monuments have largely been replaced in Adamawa by either French colonial examples, based on church architecture, or contemporary reinforced concrete examples borrowing from an international Islamic vocabulary.

**Figure 8**
Friday Mosque of Dinguiraye, Guinea, plan. Ca. 1900. Famechon, *Notice sur la Guinée Française*, p. 165.

A large central pillar, flanked by numerous smaller wood poles dividing the interior floor plan into rows and aisles, supports the earthen ceiling. The central pillar supports above it an upturned umbrella-like collection of wood poles radiating out and supporting a massive thatched domical roof that protects the earthen cube below. Such a support system for the roof is unnecessary in ordinary residential architecture due to the smaller space covered, but here it is required to prevent the rafters from bowing. The eaves extend down to a circle of short wood poles planted in a circular plan around the internal cube, cloaking the interior in deep, dark shadows much like the palace of Ngaoundéré. The mosque of Dinguiraye may therefore be characterized as a circular plan roof focused on the central pillar of a square-plan building. The persistence of the cone on cube paradigm halfway across the African continent seems from a purely formal point of view to lend credence to the theory of a pan-Fulbe architectural vocabulary.

## *Identity and Roof Form*

The architectural historian is confronted with similar styles of architecture in Guinea and Cameroon, separated by some 1,700 miles. From

**Figure 9**

Man wearing an *mbuloore*. Guassanguel, Cameroon. Photo by Mark D. DeLancey, 2000.

the perspective of a number of specifically Fulbe sources in Adamawa, there is little question that architecture is perceived as a marker of Fulbe identity, ultimately suggesting a connection with their brethren in the Fouta Djallon. On a number of occasions, Fulbe individuals in Adamawa proclaimed to me that the architectural finial is a public declaration of Fulbe identity by emulating the form of the pastoral hat known in Fulfulde as an *mbuloore* (figure 9). Like the roof finial in Ngaoundéré, the *mbuloore* covers and protects the head from the elements with a conical form created of grass fibers that comes to an emphatic point. As will ultimately be shown, however, such contemporary formulations of identity can be, and in this case are, built on objectively false presumptions.

The identification of roof cap with *mbuloore* and Fulbe identity draws upon a pride in animal husbandry, and a frequently nomadic past, that is a commonly cited element of Fulbe identity by the Fulbe themselves, as well as by researchers. The founding of Ngaoundéré, as with the rest of the polities of northern Cameroon, is traced locally to the influx of Fulbe in the early nineteenth century seeking out new pastures for their herds of cattle. A historic landmark near the center of the city is a large tree to which the city's founder, Ardo Ndjobdi, is said to have tied his calf rope. The history of pastoralism and transhumance is commonly contrasted with the culture of the indigenous Mboum population conquered by the Fulbe and who were primarily sedentary agriculturalists. Similarly, anthropologist Catherine Ver Eecke reported that the herding staff, or *sauru*, is a visible sign of Fulbe identity in northern Nigeria, carried at all times whether currently engaged in herding or not. Moreover, she pointed out that settled Fulbe frequently own cattle herds as much to maintain a connection to their pastoral heritage as for financial or status purposes.[6] In both cases, visual imagery of animal husbandry was employed in defining Fulbe identity in contrast to the prevailing agriculturally based cultures of other local ethnicities.

This sense of the roof cap indicating Fulbe identity, however, also participates in a common shorthand in the architecture of northern Cameroon, whereby the roof finial serves to quickly and easily differentiate between groups. The role of architecture in identifying distinct groups may gain at least some impetus from the extraordinary diversity of cultures resident in the region. An example can be taken from the town of Tchéboa in North Region, about 121 miles northwest of Ngaoundéré. This town is predominantly composed of Fulbe and Bata, the Bata being the indigenous population who were conquered in the earlier nineteenth century by the Fulbe, much as were the Mboum in Ngaoundéré. A project operating since the 1980s to transplant individuals from the more desiccated Far North Region to take advantage of abundant arable land has resulted in an influx of new ethnic groups. These newcomers live together in a new neighborhood, set slightly apart from the old town. The maintenance and open declaration of distinct identities is readily apparent to even the casual observer. The houses of the old village, whether of Fulbe or Bata, are usually round with conical coverings. Most houses have a second layer of thatching stitched onto the apex of the cone to help protect this most vulnerable point. For more well-to-do households, a delicate woven netting decorates the conical roofs, on the interior and the exterior, as well as serving functionally to help hold the thatching on in the face of sometimes fierce winds (figures 10 and 11).

In contrast, the newcomers' neighborhood is dotted with slightly taller buildings with oblong cones topped with sharply pointed finials (figure

[6] Catherine Ver Eecke, "Pulaaku: Adamawa Fulbe Identity and Its Transformations" (Ph.D. dissertation, University of Pennsylvania, Philadelphia, 1988), 63.

**Figure 10**
Thatched roof with woven netting at the apex. Tchéboa, Cameroon. Photo by Mark D. DeLancey, 2000.

12). Glaringly out of place in Tchéboa, these unusual roof forms are more common in the Far North Region, the point of origin of the immigrants. Thus, distinct forms of roofs, and most particularly the finials, serve to distinguish different identities in Tchéboa, much as it was suggested to me in Adamawa that conical roof finials referred to Fulbe identity by way of the *mbuloore*. That these identities are based exclusively on ethnicity rather than simply by geographic origin, however, is not clear.

## *Unitary Model of Fulbe Identity*

The similarity cited by residents of Ngaoundéré between roof-cap and pastoral Fulbe *mbuloore* resonates with similar observations by architectural historian Labelle Prussin in relation to Fulbe architecture in Fouta Djallon.[7] She suggests that the general conical form of the hat is emulated on a much larger scale by the forms of Fulbe roofs. Likewise, Prussin points out that

[7] Prussin, *Hatumere*, 82–83; Labelle Prussin, "Architectural Facets of Islam in the Futa-Djallon," in *Islamic Art and Culture in Sub-Saharan Africa*, ed. Karin Adahl (Acta Universitatis Upsaliensis, Figura Nova Series 27, Uppsala: University of Uppsala, 1995), 44–46.

**Figure 11**
Interior of roof. Tchéboa, Cameroon. Photo by Mark D. DeLancey, 2000.

**Figure 12**
Building constructed in a style typical of the Far North Region. Tchéboa, Cameroon. Photo by Mark D. DeLancey, 2000.

the circular framework woven into the inside of the hat is similar to the manner in which thatched roofs of that region are reinforced with internal rings. The points of the leather strapwork on the exterior of the *mbuloore* commonly define a four-pointed figure, recalling the square plan of the mosque of Dinguiraye. The combination of a cone with a four-pointed figure also recalls the uniting of these dichotomous forms in mosque architecture.

Prussin furthermore relates the geometric interlacing of the leather strapwork on the exterior to Islamic designs of mathematical and mystical origins, or *hatumere*, implying divine protection of the wearer. The term is a Fulfulde one that is derived from the Arabic *khatim*, or "seal." These seals, found throughout the Islamic world, are based on esoteric knowledge of the spiritual power of specific phrases from the Qurʾan, sacred names, numbers, and geometric designs. The synergistic effects of these abstract elements may be directed toward different ends, whether they be the attraction of love or success, the healing of illness, or a more general protective function.[8] While the acceptance by Islamic law of such esoteric pursuits varies in different periods and places in the Islamic world, there is little doubt that they have long held popular appeal and are widely employed in sub-Saharan Islamic cultures.

In her groundbreaking study *Hatumere*, Prussin identifies these esoteric seals as the unifying template for Islamic design across West Africa.[9] These two-dimensional geometric designs were expanded into the third dimension to create protected environments for habitation and sacred spaces for prayer. As such, the same principles applicable to the intersection of architectural design with *mbuloore* in the Fouta Djallon should theoretically also be applicable to Adamawa. Like the Fouta Djallon examples, the smooth-flowing conical roofs of palace architecture in Ngaoundéré hide an earthen cube beneath (figure 3).

Prussin asserts that the Friday Mosque of Dinguiraye, Guinea, built by the family of the legendary conqueror El Hadj Umar, is based upon a *hatumere* that he purportedly left as a plan (figure 13).[10] The *hatumere* defines a square with openings on four sides, while the corners and center are emblazoned with circular designs. The center is given particular at-

[8] See, for example, René Bravmann, "God's Secrets: Shaped in Silence," in *African Islam* (Washington, D.C.: Smithsonian Institution, 1983), 31–45; David Owusu-Ansah, "Prayer, Amulets, and Healing," in *The History of Islam in Africa*, ed. Nehemia Levtzion and Randall L. Pouwels (Athens: Ohio University Press, 2000), 477–88.

[9] Prussin, *Hatumere.*

[10] Ibid., 225–29.

**Figure 13**
*Hatumere* purportedly created by El Hadj Umar and employed as an architectural plan for constructing the Friday Mosque of Dinguiraye, Guinea. Photo by Labelle Prussin, 1979–80.

tention by surrounding it with a quatrefoil and superimposed square. The mosque of Dinguiraye likewise follows a square plan with a central pillar, much as the cone and brim of the *mbuloore* hide within the leather strapwork a four-pointed figure focused on the central vertical axis of the hat. The internal square and quatrefoil of the *hatumere* may be conceived as the umbrella-like supports radiating out from the central focus. The triple entrances on three sides and the mihrab niche on the fourth replicate the four openings of the *hatumere*. Thus, *mbuloore* may be related to mosque or palace by reference to the *hatumere*, with Islam and Fulbe ethnicity as the glue that holds all three together.

Fulbe popular histories in northern Cameroon directly connect Adamawa to the Fouta Djallon. In a history of the Fulbe polities of Maroua and Pette in the Far North Region, Cameroon, historian Eldridge Mohammadou recorded an account that the Wolarbe, the principal clan in Adamawa and more particularly the clan that founded and continues to rule Ngaoundéré, originated from one of the four boys, representing the four originating Fulbe clans, born to Sidi Uqba bin Nafi` (622–685 CE) and Mbajjou Manga, the daughter of a local ruler in Fouta Djallon.[11] Sidi Uqba, a general of the early Islamic empire, commenced the conquest of North Africa in 670 CE and founded an important mosque in Kairouan, Tunisia. In the account recorded by Mohammadou, the Wolarbe are declared to have ruled from Timbo, considered both the political and religious capital of the Fulbe confederacy in the Fouta Djallon, from whence they eventually migrated to Adamawa. This tale, moreover, relates the Wolarbe closely to the clan of Modibo Adama who founded the emirate of Adamawa in 1809, under which all the substates of northern Cameroon were incorporated into the Sokoto Caliphate. Modibo Adama hailed from the Baʾen clan, which is said to originate from the same son of Sidi Uqba as the Wolarbe. Thus, one might postulate that the architectural similarity between the Fouta Djallon and Adamawa is indicative of the common clan affiliation of the two populations, the role of that clan in political and religious leadership in both regions, and a sense of their direct historical connection.

The history recorded by Mohammadou gives an account for the origination of Adamawa Fulbe in the Fouta Djallon as an Islamic people. Related tales tracing the Fulbe to Sidi Uqba have also been recorded across the Fulbe diaspora by numerous authors.[12] These legends argue, in a sort of shorthand, for perceiving the Fulbe as one people, despite their many wanderings and shifts in lifestyles; some becoming rulers of far-flung empires, others tending their cattle over long-distance seasonal migrations, and still others settling to farm the land. Other Islamic groups across Af-

---

[11] Eldridge Mohammadou, *L'histoire des Peuls feroobe du Diamaré: Maroua et Pette.* Les traditions historiques des Peuls dans l'Adamaoua 1 (Niamey: Centre regional de documentation pour la tradition orale, 1970), 146–49. For a similar history, see Eldridge Mohammadou, *Ray ou Rey-Bouba: Les Yillaga de la Bénoué.* Traditions historiques des Foulbé de l'Adamâwa (Garoua: Musée dynamique du Nord-Cameroun, ONAREST, 1979), 137.

[12] Derrick J. Stenning, *Savannah Nomads: A Study of the Wodaabe Pastoral Fulani of Western Bornu Province, Northern Region, Nigeria* (London: International African Institute by the Oxford University Press, 1959), 18–20. Competing origin stories also trace the Fulbe to an origin in one way or another derived from cattle. Marguerite Dupire, *Peuls nomads: Etude descriptive des Wodaabe du Sahel Nigérien.* Travaux et mémoires de l'institut d'ethnologie, Université de Paris 64 (Paris: Institut d'ethnologie, Musée de l'Homme, 1962), 29–37; Amadou Hampate Ba and Germaine Dieterlen, *Koumen: Texte initiatique des pasteurs Peul.* Cahiers de l'Homme, N.S. 1 (Paris: Mouton, 1961), 29.

rica likewise claim descent from Sidi Uqba or from Bilal, the Ethiopian slave who was one of the earliest converts to Islam and served as muezzin for the Prophet Muhammad's budding community.[13] This story, and others like it, should not be understood as a factual accounting of Fulbe origins, but rather as an example of the common manner in which Islamized populations of Africa have linked themselves with the larger Islamic world.

In the early twentieth century, the unitary conception of Fulbe identity across the continent was accepted not just in popular Fulbe discourse, but also in scholarly discourse. Linguist Anneke Breedveld and anthropologist Mirjam De Bruijn, among others, trace this early scholarly emphasis on a unitary identity to the initial colonial encounter and the European perception of the Muslim Fulbe ruling organized states as an elite race derived from non-African roots.[14] I would add the key role of Islam in this perception, as Europeans were familiar with this religion and perceived monotheism as indicative of a superior intellect. The greater esteem in which the colonial powers held Islamic populations did not go unnoticed by the Fulbe and other African populations, and the expanded role that Islam has played in Fulbe identity in the twentieth century may be in part a politically astute reaction to this prejudice. At the same time, it should be pointed out that the identification of ethnic groups was part of a larger colonial project of distinguishing "tribes," seen as hermetically sealed cultural environments.

---

[13] David C. Conrad, "Blind Man Meets Prophet: Oral Tradition, Islam, and Funé Identity," in *Status and Identity in West Africa: Nyamakalaw of Mande*, ed. David C. Conrad and Barbara E. Frank (Bloomington: Indiana University Press, 1995), 86–132; David C. Conrad, "Islam in the Oral Traditions of Mali: Bilali and Surakata," *Journal of African History* 26 (1985): 33–49. Connections drawn through other figures, historical or mythical, may be found in the following sources: P. F. de Moraes Farias, "Pilgrimages to 'Pagan' Mecca in Mandenka Stories of Origin Reported from Mali and Guinea-Conakry," in *Discourse and Its Disguises: The Interpretation of African Oral Texts*, ed. Karen Barber and P. F. de Moraes Farias (Birmingham: Center for West African Studies, 1989), 152–70; P. F. de Moraes Faria, "'Yoruba Origins' Revisited by Muslims: An Interview with the Arokin of Oyo and a Reading of the Asl Qabaʾil Yuruba of Al-Hajj Adam al-Iluri," in *Self-Assertion and Brokerage: Early Cultural Nationalism in West Africa.* Birmingham University African Studies Series 2 (Birmingham: Centre of West African Studies, University of Birmingham, 1990), 121–22; R. S. O'Fahey, "Islam, State, and Society in Dar Fur," in *Conversion to Islam*, ed. Nehemia Levtzion (New York: Holmes and Meier, 1979), 192–93; Yusuf Fadl Hasan, "The Umayyad Genealogy of the Funj," *Sudan Notes and Records* 46 (1965): 27–32.

[14] Anneke Breedveld and Madame Mirjam De Bruijn, "L'image des Fulbe: Analyse critique de la construction du concept de pulaaku," *Cahiers d'etudes africaines* 36, no. 144 (1996): 793–95.

The "tribe" was defined by a single language proper only to it, and likewise a single material and artistic language producing what Sidney Kasfir has termed the "One Tribe One Style" paradigm of African art history. She traces the widespread scholarly acceptance of the coincidence of ethnicity and artistic style to William Fagg who considered the two clearest indicators of tribal identity to be language and material culture.[15]

Prussin's defining of distinct styles of Islamic art along ethnic lines, Manding, Fulbe, and Asante, follows in this model. While Islam is depicted as the force that ties all together, permitting exchange between systems, the specific character of each is derived from its unique pre-Islamic culture. The opening paragraph of the chapter on the Fulbe diaspora broadly defines the key elements for understanding the uniqueness of that ethnicity's visual culture:

> Fulbe-speaking peoples have been moving across a once-fertile Sahara for several millennia, populating areas as far west as the banks of the Sénégal River. Wherever they were and wherever they went they carried with them a strong sense of cultural identity grounded in an emotional attachment to the virtues of a nomadic life-style. Fulbe cosmologies and myths of origin continue to reflect this attachment to transhumance and to a previous matrilineal inheritance system, and the iconography of nomadism persists to this day, despite sedentarization and their rise to power in several parts of West Africa.[16]

She further indicates that the origins of Fulbe architecture lie in a confluence between the nomadic domical tent and the use of the dome in Islamic North Africa and Egypt, conveyed through the geometry employed in the creation of *hatumere*.

It must be kept in mind that this was but one chapter in a larger project that employed Islam as a unifying force, bringing together a number of visual traditions in particular through the *hatumere*. Such an approach bears resemblance to other works, such as René Bravmann's *African Islam*, which sought to understand artistic commonalities derived from Islam across African visual traditions.[17] The focus on finding commonalities

---

[15] Sidney Kasfir, "One Tribe, One Style? Paradigms in the Historiography of African Art," *History in Africa* 11 (1984): 171–72.

[16] Prussin, *Hatumere*, 198.

[17] René A. Bravmann, *African Islam* (Washington, D.C.: Smithsonian Institution, 1983).

in Islamic visual traditions in Africa was understandable considering that until the work of scholars such as Prussin and Bravmann, the role of Islam in sub-Saharan African art had been largely ignored. African art history having been founded primarily around the production of figural sculpture and masquerade, the presence of Islam seemingly wiped away all visual culture that defined the field as originally constituted. As African art historians tended to ignore Islamic cultures south of the Sahara, so too did Islamic art historians ignore them for being too African. Thus, scholars such as Prussin and Bravmann filled in the gap that had remained at the overlap of two fields of art history. One may, nevertheless, argue that the search for such commonalities presented the danger of relying too heavily on Islam as a source.

A similar critique of the uniformity of Islamic art and architecture has recently been leveled at that field by art historian Gülru Necipoglu. She has argued that the field of Islamic art history has imposed an artificial unity on the extraordinary diversity of visual cultures considered within its purview, accounting for variety in terms of "timeless ethno-national categories."[18] Where the study of Islamic and African art and architecture have overlapped, it would appear that many of the pitfalls of both have been united, producing the mirage of a unified Fulbe tradition spanning West and Central Africa based on ethnicity and Islam.

### *Diversity of Fulbe Identity*

Prussin's approach relies heavily on models popular until the 1980s that defined Fulbe identity primarily through language, nomadism, pastoralism, and Islam. The source of these unifying characteristics was thought to lie in *pulaaku*, the code of conduct often glossed as "Fulbe-ness." Anthropologist Elisabeth Boesen traces the conception of *pulaaku* as the fulcrum of Fulbe identity to Marguerite Dupire and Derrick J. Stenning, who wrote seminal studies on the Wodaabe Fulbe in Niger and northern Nigeria.[19] This code was defined in varying ways by different authors, including

[18] Gülru Necipoglu, "The Concept of Islamic Art: Inherited Discourses and New Approaches," *Journal of Art Historiography* 6 (June 2012): 4.

[19] Elisabeth Boesen, "Pulaaku: Sur la foulanité," in *Figures peules*, ed. Roger Botte, Jean Boutrais, and Jean Schmitz, Collection Hommes et Sociétés (Paris: Karthala, 1999), 84–85; Dupire, *Peuls nomads*, 1962; Stenning, *Savannah Nomads*, 1959.

values such as reserve, intelligence, respect, and patience.[20] The variation in the specific values mentioned from one Fulbe group to another, though largely ignored in these early studies, suggests that there are in fact distinctions in various Fulbe identities. As an example, sociologist Victor Azarya indicated that the nomadism to which Prussin declares the Fulbe to be emotionally attached is not a central value. Many Fulbe communities are in fact sedentary and have been for long periods of time. Azarya emphasizes that one must distinguish between ideas of nomadism and much more broadly valued pastoralism, as the two do not necessarily go hand in hand.[21] Anthropologist Angelo Maliki Bonfiglioli clarifies that the Wodaabe of Niger, often considered the archetype of the nomadic Fulbe, in reality resorted to a nomadic life in response to a number of pressures only in the late nineteenth century.[22] Prior to that period, they practiced a sedentary form of agro-pastoralism. Pastoralism, on the other hand, is seen as central enough to Fulbe identity that Christian Dupuy claimed the ability to trace the early widespread presence of Fulbe across the Sahel as early as the first century BCE from rock paintings of spear-bearing individuals in relation to cattle.[23]

Beginning in the 1980s, many scholars shifted focus from *pulaaku* as a single code to a reference point that is negotiated in individual situations at times to distinguish between Fulbe and neighboring groups, and at other times to distinguish between Fulbe groups themselves.[24] The discussions of Fulbe identity in the 1980s in general tended toward the conclusion that while there were certain elements that tied the Fulbe together across the diaspora, such as a cultural focus on cattle and use of Fulfulde language, local identities usually superseded these commonalities in everyday life.

---

[20] Breedveld and De Bruijn, "L'image des Fulbe," 796; Ver Eecke, *Pulaaku*, 52–66.

[21] Victor Azarya, "Sedentarization and Ethnic Identity among the Fulbe," in *Unity and Diversity of a People: The Search for Fulbe Identity*, ed. Paul K. Eguchi and Victor Azarya, Senri Ethnological Studies 35 (Osaka: National Museum of Ethnology, 1993), 41.

[22] Angelo Maliki Bonfiglioli, *Dudal: Histoire de famille et histoire de troupeau chez un groupe de Wodaabe du Niger* (Cambridge, Eng.: Cambridge University Press, 1988), 87–112.

[23] Christian Dupuy, "Les apports de l'archéologie et de l'ethnologie à la connaissance de l'histoire ancienne des Peuls," in *Figures peules*, ed. Roger Botte, Jean Boutrais, and Jean Schmitz, 53–72.

[24] Philip Burnham, *The Politics of Cultural Difference in Northern Cameroon* (Edinburgh: Edinburgh University Press, 1996; Nikolaus Schareika, "Pulaaku in Action: Words at Work in Wodaabe Clan Politics," *Ethnology* 49, no. 3 (Summer 2010): 207–27.

Indeed, regional differences are at times so apparent that some authors have argued that it makes little sense to speak of a single Fulbe people.[25]

It would seem that while some core elements of what it means to be Fulbe may persist, at times even being overemphasized to clearly delineate ethnic boundaries, a massive acculturation occurs everywhere that Fulbe move or settle. This is true of Adamawa as much as other areas across Africa. In terms of language, the Fulfulde of Adamawa Region incorporates significant Hausa vocabulary, as well as Mboum and other local languages. A popular characterization of this linguistic acculturation is commonly quoted in northern Cameroon: Fulfulde arrived in Maroua (in the Far North Region) in good health, fell sick in Garoua (in North Region), and died in Ngaoundéré (in Adamawa Region).

By the 1990s, *pulaaku* as a code of social mores was reconceptualized as contingent on specific exigencies to an extent that it makes little sense to attempt to define it as a single concept. *Pulaaku* was perceived as something that was formed through lived experience, rather than an ideal to which one did or did not subscribe.[26] In order to study *pulaaku*, it would not suffice to comprehend the verbal presentation of the concept, but rather it must be experientially apprehended as practiced. Specific local circumstances or situations were found to foreground particular aspects of Fulbe identity. In northern Cameroon, Islam became one of the aspects that historically distinguished the Fulbe as flag-bearers of the Sokoto Caliphate.[27] Somewhat ironically, this commonly expressed aspect of *pulaaku* is employed to distinguish the Fulbe conquerors not only from the indigenous population, but also from those Fulbe, known as Mbororo, who maintained a transhumant pastoral life. The Mbororo were, and still are, looked down upon as uncouth, simple, untrustworthy, and lax in their command of Islam, if not outright pagan. As with more recent research

[25] See especially Paul K. Eguchi and Victor Azarya, eds., *Unity and Diversity of a People: The Search for Fulbe Identity*, Senri Ethnological Studies 35 (Osaka: National Museum of Ethnology, 1993). The articles in this text all address the issue of Fulbe identity, some arguing for a common identity and some against. The malleability of Fulbe identity across the diaspora and over time is an important subject of many of these essays. Likewise, a collection of essays by the participants in the GRÉFUL (Groupe d'études comparatives des societies peules) gatherings of scholars in France also dwells on issues of Fulbe identity: Roger Botte, Jean Boutrais, and Jean Schmitz, eds., *Figures peules*, Collection Hommes et Sociétés (Paris: Karthala, 1999).

[26] Boesen, "Pulaaku"; Shareika, "Pulaaku in Action," 207–27.

[27] Burnham, *Politics of Cultural Difference*, 48–53.

on Fulbe identity in general, one would expect a similar interest in local permutations and negotiations of what constitutes Fulbe architecture, if indeed any such thing can be defined in a particular locale.

Boesen has broached such an approach with respect to nomadic Fulbe visual culture of the Wodaabe of Niger. She draws attention to the essentially consumerist orientation of the Wodaabe, who have quite willingly incorporated aspects in particular of Tuareg culture as well as select industrial products. She determines that modern products that essentially fulfill culturally predefined needs that the Wodaabe are unable or unwilling to satisfy with their own labor are most widely adopted.[28] In Adamawa and elsewhere, the adoption of local architecture by sedentary Fulbe, particularly when fashioned by hired local labor, exemplifies a similar mode of adoption to that of the Wodaabe.

### *Adopting Architecture*

In terms of the arts, some elements, such as the *mbuloore*, may be maintained, though perhaps filtered through local visual traditions. Barbara Frank expresses the false identification in the Malian context of specific forms with specific cultures by suggesting that the profession of the patron or identity of the artist may be just as key to understanding its references. She takes the example of the *mbuloore*, stating that it is "usually identified in museum records as Fulani and worn by Fula and other herdsmen out in the hot sun, [but that it] may just as easily have been adorned by a Dogon or Bamana leatherworker as a Fula one."[29] Likewise, one may find other ethnicities performing a similar pastoral occupation wearing the *mbuloore*. Thus, what has been characterized as a clear referent to Fulbe identity is in reality a nexus of cultural intersections in its design, creation, and employment.

Other art forms such as permanent architecture, for which semi-nomadic pastoral Fulbe had no immediate precedent, might be borrowed wholesale. This corresponds to a central theory of Victor Azarya's comparative study of Fulbe in Guinea, Nigeria, and Cameroon.[30] In those areas such as

---

[28] Elisabeth Boesen, "Gleaming like the Sun: Values in Wodaabe Material Culture," *Africa* 78, no. 4 (2008), 583–86.

[29] Barbara E. Frank, *Mande Potters and Leatherworkers: Art and Heritage in West Africa* (Washington, D.C.: Smithsonian Institution, 1998), 150.

[30] Victor Azarya, *Aristocrats Facing Change: The Fulbe in Guinea, Nigeria, and Cameroon* (Chicago: University of Chicago Press, 1978).

Guinea and Cameroon where the Fulbe created a political system largely *ex novo*, their culture has been vigorously maintained and elements of it have been adopted by the local population. In cases such as northern Nigeria, where the Fulbe inherited preexisting state structures, they acculturated so completely that it became difficult to distinguish Fulbe from non-Fulbe. This model could be more nuanced, for even the state structures that the Fulbe introduced in some areas must be understood as having been adopted from elsewhere. In the case of Adamawa, which so far as is known was previously composed of a large number of small-scale polities, the Fulbe set up new state structures based on the model of the Sokoto Caliphate of northern Nigeria, into which northern Cameroon was integrated in the early nineteenth century. The Sokoto Caliphate's political system was in turn a combination of prior Hausa structures with models drawn from the early Islamic Caliphate. At the same time, the previously nomadic Fulbe in Adamawa adopted local architecture and other cultural elements for which they had no precedents in their own culture.

Azarya's general concept of the Fulbe at times adopting novel cultural features from local populations was by no means a recent one, but simply one that was laid aside for some time. As early as 1906, J. Machat in writing about the Fouta Djallon region of Guinea explained that settled Fulbe frequently adopt elements of the sedentary cultures among whom they take up residence.[31] This idea of cultural adoption is in tension with the more generalized early twentieth-century perception of a common Fulbe identity. More specifically relating to architecture, the 1952 publication *L'habitat au Cameroun* presented the research of seven French architects who visited the country with the aim of understanding the local architecture and gaining insights for the development of culturally and climatically appropriate modern architecture. The result was an extraordinary collection of drawings and photographs, accompanied by a horribly paternalistic text. For northern Cameroon, a strict division was drawn between the mountains and the plains, with an entirely separate section for the Fulbe. The peoples of the mountains, so-called *montagnards*, were described as picturesque, yet unhygienic, noble-savage types who had resisted outside influences whether of Fulbe or European origin. The peoples of the plains, on the other hand, were perceived to have largely capitulated to Fulbe culture after a century of slave raids and conquests. The Fulbe were portrayed

[31] J. Machat, *Guinée française: Les rivières du sud et le Fouta Diallon: Géographie physique et civilisations indigènes* (Paris: Augustin Challamel, 1906), 274.

as militant conquerors who reside largely in the cities. The architecture of the Fulbe was described essentially as adopted from the local populations wherever they settled, much as suggested by Machat for the Fouta Djallon.[32] The nature of this borrowing, however, was never defined very well either in the text or in the images.

The view of the Fulbe as cultural borrowers was echoed only fifteen years later by art historian and anthropologist Jacqueline Delange who referred to the Fulbe as "fundamentally borrowers of techniques" in whose culture, "borrowing itself has its own philosophy."[33] Delange furthermore mused that the geometric designs decorating Fulbe architecture of the Fouta Djallon are of Islamic origin. She asserts, however, that the Islamic-derived decoration should in fact be ascribed to the Mande artists who created it, rather than to the Fulbe who commissioned the work. Similarly, she points out that the Fulbe adopted earthen architecture for reasons of prestige and comfort from local populations in Mali, Burkina Faso, and northern Cameroon.[34] Like the authors of *L'habitat au Cameroun*, Delange gave little in the way of specific examples that might demonstrate this borrowing either in text or in image. Delange's statement that borrowing is a philosophy of its own for the Fulbe, despite the paucity of examples furnished, was nevertheless quite insightful.

The division between mountains and plains put forth in *L'habitat au Cameroun* was picked up in the later writings of geographer Christian Seignobos, who conflates the two categories with those of pagan *montagnards* and Fulbe.[35] His published work stresses the distinctiveness of *montagnard* models from those of the Fulbe, encouraging a harder-edged definition of ethnicity and architectural style. Non-Fulbe peoples who live on the plains are dealt with by Seignobos, but are understood simply as permutations of *montagnards*. The artificiality of the distinction is most apparent when treating the architecture of peoples who completely surround predominantly Fulbe settlements, yet the central Fulbe settlements are ignored. Such is the case, for example, with his brief treat-

---

[32] *L'habitat au Cameroun* (Paris: Publications de la recherche scientifique outre-mer; Editions de l'union française, 1952), 59.

[33] Jacqueline Delange, *The Art and Peoples of Black Africa* (New York: E. P. Dutton, 1974), 140–41. The original French edition was published in 1967.

[34] Ibid., 144–45.

[35] In particular, see Christian Seignobos, *Nord Cameroun: Montagnes et hautes terres,* Collection architectures traditionnelles (Roquevaire, France: Editions parenthèses, 1982).

ment of Di'i, Mboum, and Gbaya architecture of Adamawa, while ignoring the Fulbe-dominated city of Ngaoundéré entirely.[36] The Fulbe were left for a second volume, *Plaines du Nord-Cameroun*, which was unfortunately never published. Seignobos's description of his intentions is telling, however, of his theoretical dependency on the earlier work of *L'habitat au Cameroun*. He states that the intended second volume will present a more impoverished catalog of types, just as the ethnic profile is radically simplified. He goes on to say, however, that it is in the capitals of the Islamic states that one finds the most acculturation and architectural changes that have produced contemporary architectural models.[37] This declaration directly echoes the stated raison d'être of *L'habitat au Cameroun*.

One of the most recent works on Fulbe architecture, though outside of Cameroon, is by architect Jean-Paul Bourdier and filmmaker Trinh T. Minh-ha.[38] Their book includes a chapter, along with two visual essays, on Fulbe architecture in a broader study of Senegalese architecture. On the one hand, the authors acknowledge, in both text and images, the diversity of traditions even within one nation. On the other hand, through an overreliance on the works of Fulbe scholar Ahmadou Hampaté Ba as the sole interpretative lens, they reimpose a unity of interpretation upon what is clearly a diverse visual tradition. This restrictive lens amounts to an essentialist focus on the pastoral nomadic existence that is commonly considered the font of Fulbe culture, as explicitly affirmed by the authors, and just as explicitly contradicted by Bonfiglioli. More permanent architecture is treated, however, toward the end of the chapter in which the authors briefly examine the intersection of Fulbe architecture with that of their Malinke, Jaxanke, Soninke, and Tukulor neighbors. One is left with a lack of clarity regarding the orientation of the authors with respect to the issue of defining what exactly constitutes Fulbe architecture.

In the rather undeveloped literature on Fulbe architecture, it becomes clear that most who wrote on the subject generally recognized a diversity

[36] Ibid., 169–81.

[37] Ibid., 12.

[38] *Drawn from African Dwellings* (Bloomington: Indiana University Press, 1996), 22–71, 116–29. There are also two chapters on the architecture of the Tokolor, considered by many as part of the larger Fulbe culture. Ibid., 72–115, 134–83.

of architectural forms across the many areas that the Fulbe settled. As a result of shifts from transhumant to sedentary life, the temporary shelter of the nomad was discarded in favor of more permanent structures. That said, other explanations, including ethnic specialization in particular sectors of production, intermarriage, slavery, the environment, and still other factors must be considered as possibly responsible for the adoption of architectural forms by the Fulbe. In any case, the diversity of styles represented in these permanent structures points to the adoption of local forms rather than a basis in nomadic, pastoral, Islamic, or even particularly Fulbe values that might produce greater uniformity across the diaspora.

### *Northern Cameroonian Architecture of the Fulbe*

Refocusing attention from the Fulbe diaspora and the glue that is Islam to the local context suggests that there is in fact little that can be defined as specifically Fulbe or necessarily Islamic about Fulbe architecture in northern Cameroon, beyond perhaps the obvious necessities of a mosque. The roofing system used in Adamawa, while similar in some respects to that of the Fouta Djallon, also conforms closely to techniques seen among other populations of Cameroon. At the Mboum palace of Ngangha, 25 miles northeast of Ngaoundéré, the roof of the cubical entrance building is roughly conical, much like that of the palace of Ngaoundéré (figure 14). In climbing up into the roof, I discovered that it was supported by an internal pyramidal reinforcing framework fastened to the outer pyramidal armature (figure 15).[39] Such a reinforcing framework would prevent bowing of the roof, helping it to maintain its general form. The outer pyramidal form, as at Ngaoundéré, is softened into a rounded form on the exterior with thatching and the use of porches.

The principles employed at Ngangha and Ngaoundéré are also similar to those used in the architecture of the Cameroon Grasslands to the southwest, despite differing materials. The Grasslands covers areas of the Northwest, Southwest, and West Regions of Cameroon. It is home to numerous kingdoms, none of which are Fulbe and with Islam a predominant faith only in Bamum. At Bandjoun, as exemplified by both a woman's

---

[39] It should be noted that this internal framework is distinct from that shown in a cutaway diagram of the same building by Seignobos. Seignobos, *Nord Cameroun*, 179.

**Figure 14**
Palace, entrance. Ngangha, Cameroon. Photo by Mark D. DeLancey, 2000.

**Figure 15**

Palace, internal reinforcing framework of the roof of the entrance. Ngangha, Cameroon. Photo by Mark D. DeLancey, 2000.

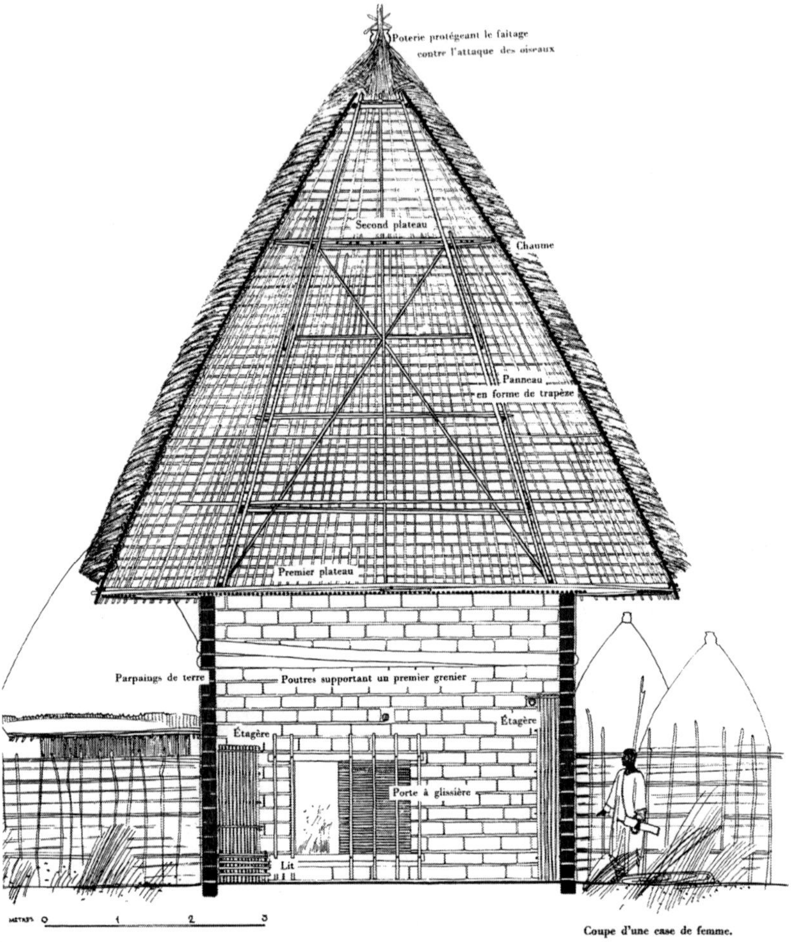


**Figure 16**

Section of a woman's residence showing the internal roof support system. *L'habitat au Cameroun*, p. 84. Reproduced with the permission of L'Institut de Recherche pour le Développement.

residence and the grand council chamber in the palace, a cubical room is covered by a circular ceiling, itself surmounted by a pyramidal framework (figures 16 and 17). A second disc, similar to but smaller than the ceiling, is added near the top of the pyramidal framework. An external conical framework is then bound to the internal form at the levels of the

**Figure 17**
Palace, Council chamber, Bandjoun, Cameroon. Photo by Mark D. DeLancey, 1996.

ceiling, disc, and apex. Finally thatching is added to create the finished, rain-resistant roof.[40] This system is very similar to, though perhaps more sophisticated than, that observed at Ngangha.

Ironically, the upturned umbrella-like support structure seen in Fouta Djallon, while not employed in Adamawa, is also used in the Grasslands architectural tradition.[41] There is little to directly connect the use of such internal roof supports in the Grasslands to the Fouta Djallon either in terms of ethnicity or religion. Instead, its use is best considered as one logical means of supporting the tall and acutely slanted roofs employed in response to the heavy rainfall experienced in these locales.

Common environmental factors may be at least partly responsible for perceived similarities between Adamawa, the Grasslands, and the Fouta Djallon. These three areas are characterized by mountainous topography, with relatively heavy rainfall in both areas. Rainfall in the Fouta Djallon, depending on the specific location, ranges from 60 to 100 inches

---

[40] *L'habitat*, 79–87.

[41] Wolfgang Lauber, *Palaces and Compounds in the Grasslands of Cameroon* (Stuttgart: Karl Krämer Verlag, 1990), 26.

annually, primarily between June and September.[42] The same average rainfall is recorded for the Cameroon Grasslands. While less, the area around Ngaoundéré also receives significant rainfall amounting to approximately 59 inches annually between April and October. This amount is twice the annual rainfall of the low-lying Far North Region, where buildings may lack a thatched roof altogether.[43] Thus, one environmentally deterministic interpretation for the heavy thatching and extensive eaves in the Fouta Djallon, Adamawa, and the Grasslands may be as a means of protection from the rain, and in particular to avoid erosion of the unbaked earthen walls.

The interior supports of the ceilings differ between northern Cameroon and the Fouta Djallon. While there may be a number of supports for Fouta Djallon structures, the central one is stressed with increased size and decoration. It is this pillar which supports the upturned umbrella form that helps to maintain the integrity of the roof. In contrast, Adamawa structures of a similar grandeur feature rows of pillars, normally four or six, leading back from the entrance. No one pillar is emphasized more than the other and none specifically carries the roof above.[44]

Likewise, the external supports of the eaves differ between the two regions, and result in a more uniformly conical roof in the Fouta Djallon. To create the eaves in Adamawa, a series of wood posts, longer in the center and decreasing in height toward the ends, are placed in a semicircular plan before the façade (figure 18). Thatching is then extended from the surface of the roof over the framework to cover a small porch in front of the wall (figure 19). It is this supplementary extension of the roofline that gives the architecture of Ngaoundéré its gentle undulation as one moves around the structure. These roofs, built by the Fulbe as well as Mboum and others, differ significantly in plan and surface quality from the roofs of structures in the Fouta Djallon, which feature an entire circle of stakes around the cubical core and hence a more regular conical form.

---

[42] Harold D. Nelson et. al., *Area Handbook for Guinea* (Washington, D.C.: U.S. Government Printing Office, 1975), 47.

[43] Harold D. Nelson et. al., *Area Handbook for the United Republic of Cameroon* (Washington, D.C.: U.S. Government Printing Office, 1975), 44–46.

[44] This is in contrast with the palace of Bandjoun, where the roof of the main communal structure is supported by a single large pillar. This pillar serves as a metaphor for the ruler as fulcrum for the kingdom. See Dominique Malaquais, "Constructing Power: Architecture, Landscape, and the Design of Space in a Chieftaincy of the Bamileke Highlands" (Ph.D. dissertation, Columbia University, New York, 1997), 90–93.

**Figure 18**

Framework for the porch of a Mboum residence. Mbang-Mboum, Cameroon. Photo by Mark D. DeLancey, 2000.

The commonly espoused ethnic specificity of the roof cap in Adamawa presents similar questions. If the roof cap were primarily a symbol of Fulbe ethnicity, then one would expect to find it solely on Fulbe roofs. Such is emphatically not the case, however, as the Mboum, Diʾi, and other ethnicities in the region all build steeply pitched roofs with roof caps, given the means. One could argue that this represents the general Fulbeization of the population, a process which has indeed been documented in northern Cameroon identity politics, but I would argue that the roof cap is too prevalent to make this case. Instead, its geographical specificity to Ngaoundéré and its environs, rather than a Fulbe identity, suggests a primary denotation of local rather than ethnic identity.

On a local level, the identification of this style of architecture specifically with the Fulbe, or even a category that one could call Fulbe architecture, is quickly disputed by the historically indigenous Mboum and Diʾi populations. The Mboum ruler, or *bellaka*, of Mbang-Mboum, 22 miles northeast of Ngaoundéré, asked me when I queried him about the Fulbe palace of Ngaoundéré if I had ever seen Fulbe architecture. Had I seen their little grass huts, clearly referring to the frame tents of semi-nomadic Fulbe? He affirmed his belief that the Fulbe do not truly have architecture,

**Figure 19**
Palace, eaves of the west porch of the second building (*Jawleeru Njakmukon*). Ngaoundéré, Cameroon. Photo by Mark D. DeLancey, 2000.

but rather that it is the Mboum who built the palace of Ngaoundéré for them. Similarly, a Mboum servant of the ruler of Ngaoundéré and his friends angrily rejected the title of the 1978 doctoral dissertation of geographer André Gondolo that I showed them entitled *Ngaoundéré: Evolution of a Fulbe City*.[45] Instead, they insisted that Ngaoundéré is a Mboum city in which the Fulbe were permitted to settle.

In fact, the official charged with all construction at the palace of Ngaoundéré is the Kaygama Mboum, or Mboum representative at court. The workforce for construction and repairs within the palace is chosen from among the Mboum population. The majority of the inhabitants of the palace—wives, concubines, servants, and guards—are of Mboum ethnicity. The language of the palace is by and large Mboum and the buildings are referred to by Mboum names. The ruler himself is historically required to be of the royal family on his father's side, but to have a Mboum mother.[46] Indeed, both Fulbe and Mboum readily acknowledge that the site of Ngaoundéré was formerly the location of a Mboum capital, and that the Fulbe were initially invited to settle there by the Mboum ruler. The name Ngaoundéré itself is a compound Mboum term meaning "Mountain of the Navel," referencing the unusually shaped mountain below which the city was established.

The roof cap clearly does not serve to distinguish ethnicity in Adamawa Region. In addition, it is absent outside of that specific area, even where dominated by the same Fulbe clan. The town of Boundang-Touroua, located 130 miles northwest of Ngaoundéré and only 15 miles west of Tchéboa, illustrates this lack of continuity. Boundang-Touroua, like its proximate neighbor, is populated largely by Bata and Fulbe from the Wollarbe clan. The town was founded by the Wollarbe in the late eighteenth century and remained an important capital city until Ngaoundéré was founded in approximately 1835. Thereafter, Boundang-Touroua was reduced to a provincial town under the control of Ngaoundéré, and governed by a branch of Ngaoundéré's royal family, until the two were administratively separated by the German colonial regime in 1914. Despite

[45] André Gondolo, *N'Gaoundéré: Evolution d'une ville peul* (Ph.D. dissertation, Université de Rouen, 1978).

[46] In actual practice, the rule that a ruler's mother be Mboum is not always followed, though she is always from one of the indigenous non-Fulbe groups. Anthropologist Ketil Fred Hansen briefly discusses this issue in his doctoral dissertation. *The Historical Construction of a Political Culture in Ngaoundere, Northern Cameroon,* Faculty of Arts 81 (Oslo: University of Oslo, 2000), 96.

the common clan affiliation and direct historical connection, the forms of roofs in Boundang-Touroua are quite distinct from those of Ngaoundéré, and bear a greater similarity to those at Tchéboa (figures 20 and 10). Thus, the roof cap and particular form of roofs of elite architecture in Ngaoundéré and surrounding areas must be understood as a signifier of local identity irrespective of ethnicity.

## *Conclusion*

In a field such as African architecture that is so diverse, it is appealing and necessary to find broader convergences. Scholars have suggested that Islam and common ethnicity can provide some of that long-distance cohesion across the Fulbe diaspora. In focusing exclusively on these elements, however, both art-producing populations as well as scholars may be complicit. For the Fulbe of Adamawa, stressing pan-Fulbe and Islamic identities, and in particular relationships with the Fouta Djallon, may be a modern strategy of differentiation on a local level in a struggle for government recognition. This is a struggle that commenced in the colonial era when Islamic groups were considered more evolved and thus more capable of governing both themselves and surrounding non-Islamic groups. It is a struggle which has persisted into the postcolonial era, as has been documented for the Far North Region.[47]

For scholars, common ethnicity and religious background would seemingly provide the explanation for the appearance of similar forms at opposite ends of the Fulbe diaspora. Yet scholars must beware of jumping to the conclusion of a direct relationship based simply on formal similarities, just as they must not allow the presence of a common ethnicity or religion across broad distances to blind them to crosscurrents with other cultures, which may or may not be Islamic, on a local level. Ethnic and religious categories may well bear less meaning than local identities, or may constitute more recent reinterpretations under shifting political and sociocultural forces. In the specific case of Cameroon, Islam and the Fulbe presence are important factors that have led scholars to rigidly divide the north of the country from the south, and to subdivide the north into Fulbe and non-Fulbe. This rigid

[47] Diane Lyons, "The Politics of House Shape: Round vs. Rectilinear in Northern Cameroon," *Antiquity* 70, no. 268 (June 1996): 364–67; Kees Schilder, *Quest for Self-Esteem: State, Islam, and Mundang Ethnicity in Northern Cameroon,* Research Series 1994/3 (Leiden: African Studies Centre, 1994).

**Figure 20**

Entrance to a residence. Boundang-Touroua, Cameroon. Photo by Mark D. DeLancey, 2000.

division was imposed on the basis of a preexisting colonial-era supposition, rather than on actual cultural evidence. The consideration of local cultures and identities within which differences in ethnic identities and religious persuasion may occur provides a means by which one can begin to connect the different provinces of Cameroon which have until now been considered so divorced. Building an inclusive local history of architecture is a necessity in combatting the often artificial divisions invoked, or provoked, in the colonial period that continue to haunt the present.

## *Bibliography*

Azarya, Victor. *Aristocrats Facing Change: The Fulbe in Guinea, Nigeria, and Cameroon*. Chicago: University of Chicago Press, 1978.

———. "Sedentarization and Ethnic Identity among the Fulbe." In *Unity and Diversity of a People: The Search for Fulbe Identity*, edited by Paul K. Eguchi and Victor Azarya, 35–60. Senri Ethnological Studies 35. Osaka: National Museum of Ethnology, 1993.

Ba, Amadou Hampate, and Germaine Dieterlen. *Koumen: Texte initiatique des Pasteurs Peul*. Cahiers de l'Homme, N.S. 1. Paris: Mouton, 1961.

Boesen, Elisabeth. "Des localités nomades: Les 'maisons' Wodaabe en brousse et en ville." In *Les nouveaux urbains dans l'espace Sahara-Sahel*, edited by Elisabeth Boesen and Laurence Marfaing, 209–31. Paris: Karthala, 2007.

———. "Gleaming Like the Sun: Aesthetic Values in Wodaabe Material Culture." *Africa* 78, no. 4 (2008): 582–602.

———. "*Pulaaku*: Sur la foulanité." In *Figure peules*, edited by Roger Botte, Jean Boutrais, and Jean Schmitz, 83–97. Paris: Karthala, 1999.

Bonfiglioli, Angelo Maliki. *Dudal: Histoire de famille et historie du troupeau chez un groupe de Wodaabe du Niger*. Cambridge, Eng.: Cambridge University Press, 1988.

Botte, Roger, Jean Boutrais, and Jean Schmitz. *Figures peules*. Paris: Karthala, 1999.

Bravmann, René. *African Islam*. Washington, D.C.: Smithsonian Institution, 1983.

Breedveld, Anneke, and Mirjam De Bruijn. "L'image des Fulbe: Analyse critique de la construction du concept de pulaaku." *Cahiers d'études africaines* 36, no. 144 (1996): 791–821.

Burnham, Philip. *The Politics of Cultural Difference in Northern Cameroon*. Washington, D.C.: Smithsonian Institution, 1996.

Conrad, David C. "Blind Man Meets Prophet: Oral Tradition, Islam, and *Funé* Identity." In *Status and Identity in West Africa*: Nyamakalaw *of Mande*, edited by David C. Conrad and Barbara E. Frank, 86–132. Bloomington: Indiana University Press, 1995.

———. "Islam in the Oral Traditions of Mali: Bilali and Surakata." *Journal of African History* 26 (1985): 33–49.

Creac'h, P. "Notes sur l'art décoratif architectural Foula du haut Fouta-Djallon." In *Comptes rendus de la première conférence internationale des africanistes de l'ouest*, 300–312. Paris: Librairie d'Amérique et d'Orient Adrien-Maisonneuve, 1951.

DeLancey, Mark D. "The Spread of the Sooro: Symbols of Rulership in the Sokoto Empire." *Journal of the Society of Architectural Historians* 71, no. 2 (June 2012): 68–85.

Delange, Jacqueline. *The Art and Peoples of Black Africa*. New York: E. P. Dutton, 1974.

Diallo, Thierno. "Origine et migration des peuls avant le XIXe siècle." *Annales de la faculté des lettres et sciences humaines* 2 (1972): 121–74.

Dupire, Marguerite. *Peuls nomads: Etude descriptive des Wodaabe du Sahel Nigérien*. Travaux et mémoires de l'institut d'ethnologie, Université de Paris 64. Paris: Institut d'ethnologie, Musée de l'Homme, 1962.

Dupuy, Christian. "Les apports de l'archéologie et de l'ethnologie à la connaissance de l'histoire ancienne des Peuls." In *Figure peules*, edited by Roger Botte, Jean Boutrais, and Jean Schmitz, 53–72. (Paris: Karthala, 1999).

Eguchi, Paul K., and Victor Azarya, eds., *Unity and Diversity of a People: The Search for Fulbe Identity*. Senri Ethnological Studies 35. Osaka: National Museum of Ethnology, 1993.

Famechon, M. *Notice sur la Guinée Française*. Colonies et pays de protectorats. Paris: Comité Local de l'Exposition & M. Victor Gaboriaud, 1900.

Frank, Barbara E. *Mande Potters and Leatherworkers: Art and Heritage in West Africa*. Washington, D.C.: Smithsonian Institution, 1998.

Gondolo, André. *N'Gaoundéré: Evolution d'une ville peul*. Ph.D. dissertation, Université de Rouen, Rouen, 1978.

Hansen, Ketil Fred. *The Historical Construction of a Political Culture in Ngaoundere, Northern Cameroon*. Faculty of Arts 81. Ph.D. dissertation, University of Oslo, Oslo, 2000.

Hasan, Yusuf Fadl. "The Umayyad Genealogy of the Funj." *Sudan Notes and Records* 46 (1965): 27–32.

Kasfir, Sidney Littlefield. "One Tribe, One Style? Paradigms in the Historiography of African Art." *History in Africa* 11 (1984): 163–93.

Kreamer, Christine Mullen. *Inscribing Meaning: Writing and Graphic Systems in African Art*. Washington, D.C.: Smithsonian Institution, 2007.

Lauber, Wolfgang. *Palaces and Compounds in the Grasslands of Cameroon: Traditional Wood Architecture of a West African Country*. Stuttgart: Karl Krämer Verlag, 1990.

*L'habitat au Cameroun*. Paris: Publications de la recherche scientifique outre-mer; Editions de l'union française, 1952.

Lyons, Diane. "The Politics of House Shape: Round vs. Rectilinear in Northern Cameroon." *Antiquity* 70, no. 268 (June 1996): 351–67.

Machat, J. *Guinée française: Les rivières du sud et le Fouta Diallon: Géographie physique et civilisations indigènes*. Paris: Augustin Challamel, 1906.

Malaquais, Dominique. "Constructing Power: Architecture, Landscape, and the Design of Space in a Chieftaincy of the Bamileke Highlands." Ph.D. dissertation, Columbia University, New York, 1997.

Mohammadou, Eldridge. *L'histoire des Peuls feroobe du Diamaré: Maroua et Pette*. Les Traditions Historiques des Peuls dans l'Adamaoua 1. Niamey: Centre régional de documentation pour la tradition orale, 1970.

———. *Ray ou Rey-Bouba: Les Yillaga de la Bénoué*. Traditions historiques des Foulbé de l'Adamâwa. Garoua: Musée dynamique du Nord-Cameroun, ONAREST, 1979.

Moraes Farias, P. F. de. "Pilgrimages to 'Pagan' Mecca in Mandenka Stories of Origin Reported from Mali and Guinea-Conakry." In *Discourse and Its Disguises: The Interpretation of African Oral Texts*, edited by Karen Barber and P. F. de Moraes Farias, 152–70. Birmingham: Center for West African Studies, 1989.

———. "'Yoruba Origins' Revisited by Muslims: An Interview with the *Arokin* of Oyo and a Reading of the *Asl Qaba'il Yuruba* of *Al-Hajj* Adam al-Iluri." In *Self-Assertion and Brokerage: Early Cultural Nationalism in West Africa*, 109–47. Birmingham University African Studies Series 2. Birmingham: Centre of West African Studies: University of Birmingham, 1990.

Necipoglu, Gülru. "The Concept of Islamic Art: Inherited Discourses and New Approaches." *Journal of Art Historiography* 6 (June 2012): 6-GN/1.

Nelson, Harold D., et al. *Area Handbook for Guinea*. Washington, D.C.: U.S. Government Printing Office, 1975.

———. *Area Handbook for the United Republic of Cameroon*. Washington, D.C.: U.S. Government Printing Office, 1975.

Nelson, Steven. *From Cameroon to Paris: Mousgoum Architecture in & out of Africa*. Chicago: University of Chicago Press, 2007.

O'Fahey, R. S. "Islam, State, and Society in Dar Fur." In *Conversion to Islam*, edited by Nehemia Levtzion, 189–206. New York: Holmes and Meier, 1979.

Owusu-Ansah, David. "Prayer, Amulets, and Healing." In *The History of Islam in Africa*, edited by Nehemia Levtzion and Randall L. Pouwels, 477–88. Athens: Ohio University Press, 2000.

Poujade, Jean. *Les cases décorées d'un chef du Fouta Djiallo*. Documents d'ethnographie terrestre 1. Paris: Gauthier-Villars, 1948.

Prussin, Labelle. "Architectural Facets of Islam in the Futa-Djallon." In *Islamic Art and Culture in Sub-Saharan Africa*, edited by Karin Adahl, 21–56. Acta Universitatis Upsaliensis, Figura Nova Series 27. Uppsala: University of Uppsala, 1995.

———. *Hatumere: Islamic Design in West Africa*. Berkeley: University of California Press, 1986.

———. "Sub-Saharan West Africa." In *The Mosque: History, Architectural Development & Regional Diversity*, edited by Martin Frishman and Hasan-Uddin Khan, 180–93. London: Thames and Hudson, 1994.

Schareika, Nikolaus. "Pulaaku in Action: Words at Work in Wodaabe Clan Politics." *Ethnology* 49, no. 3 (Summer 2010): 207–27.

Schilder, Kees. *Quest for Self-Esteem: State, Islam, and Mundang Ethnicity in Northern Cameroon*. Research Series 1994/3. Leiden: African Studies Centre, 1994.

Seignobos, Christian. *Nord Cameroun: Montagnes et hautes terres*. Collection Architectures traditionnelles. Roquevaire, France: Editions parenthèses, 1982.

Stenning, Derrick J. *Savannah Nomads: A Study of the Wodaabe Pastoral Fulani of Western Bornu Province, Northern Region, Nigeria*. London: International African Institute by the Oxford University Press, 1959.

Ver Eecke, Catherine. "Pulaaku: Adamawa Fulbe Identity and Its Transformations." Ph.D. dissertation, University of Pennsylvania, Philadelphia, 1988.

# Negotiating Islamic Revival: Public Religiosity in Nouakchott City

*Elemine Ould Mohamed Baba Moustapha,* NOUAKCHOTT *UNIVERSITY*

DOI: 10.5192/21540993050145

**Abstract**

*As waves of Islamism have given rise to new signs of public religiosity in Nouakchott over the last decades, it becomes relevant to wonder how a long-established Islamic tradition of Moorish society negotiates these recent Islamic currents and to study their impact on the traditional links between warriors and scholars. The main goal of this article is to characterize a specific attitude toward Islamism in Mauritania.*

There has been a striking emergence in recent decades of new signs of public religiosity in Nouakchott, Mauritania. The most fundamental question is how does a long-established Islamic tradition[1] of Moorish

[1] We can characterize the classical Islamic tradition of Moorish society as strictly based on Maliki *fiqh* in its Qassémite-Khalilian form. The bulk of this religious knowledge was reproduced through the *maḥadra* (traditional school), a unique institution among nomadic societies. The *maḥadra* were monitored by the conservative *zwāya* clans that held judicial authority, safeguarded moral values, and claimed mystical powers. See C. C. Stewart, *Islam and Social Order in Mauritania: A Case Study from the Nineteenth Century* (Oxford: Clarendon, 1973); and Y. Ould al-Bara, "Fiqh, société et pouvoir: Préoccupations et soucis des théologiens maures du XVIIème au XXème siècle" (Ph.D. diss., Ecole des Hautes Etudes en Sciences Sociales, 2000).

*Islamic Africa,* VOL. 5, NO. 1, 2014. ISSN 2154-0993.  www.islamicafricajournal.org

society[2] negotiate more recent Islamic currents, which have affected Nouakchott city predominantly throughout its *daʾwa* category.[3]

In other words, how does a practice of Islam nurtured by many centuries of a specific Saharan environment and scholarship react to the waves of Islamism that have washed across Nouakchott since the 1970s? To what extent do new forms of religious expression in Nouakchott's public space fit into the Moorish society's historical legacy? Are they acting as a complementary process or in contradiction? How do universal values mesh with locally constructed ideas about Islam?

Moreover, the sacred and profane within these expressions must be examined. To what extent, for instance, does the ancient proximity of sacred and profane and the cohabitation of warriors (*Banū Ḥassān*) and scholars (*zwāya*)[4] affect present-day modern practices of religion?

But although it is particularly difficult to accurately appreciate and measure religious behavior, I have tried to obtain some understanding of this through a survey targeting several public[5] expressions of religiosity including mosque numbers/attendance, "shouting sellers," audiocassette shops, radio/TV broadcasting, Islamic labels, and religious music. This work was conducted during the spring and summer of 2012.

I chose nine main boulevards in the city with an approximate length

---

[2] Mauritanian society includes various ethnic groups including Moors, Pulaar, Soninké, and Wolof. The emphasis of this article is on Moorish society in large part because the majority of my data comes from this group as well as my own experiences. In addition, the growth of Nouakchott during the last decades makes a complete overview difficult. Consequently this article focuses on areas of the city I know best, including the east, central, and northern sections, populated mostly by Moors (locally called Bidan).

[3] By Islamism, I mean particularly the wing linked with proselytism (*daʾwa*) that is often confused with *Tablīġi* in Mauritania and each one could stand for the other. Beyond the semiotic matter in Arabic, I follow Ould Ahmed Salem (2007) in his classification. They are generally distinguished from other more politically committed Islamists which are the moderate stream (*Tawāṣul Party*) and jihadists.

[4] Premodern, nomadic Moorish society was marked by two distinct occupational groups, one that traced descent from the Arab intruders of the seventeenth century, or *Banū Ḥassān,* and those whose genealogies were traced to indigenous, Sanhadja, or Berber peoples who identified themselves as *zwāya*. This led to a polarity between *Banū Ḥassān* political power established by the sword and the religious authority of *zwāya* sourced in knowledge and mysticism. See A.-W. Ould Cheikh, "Nomadisme, Islam et pouvoir politique dans la société maure précoloniale (XIè-XIXè)" (Ph.D. diss., Paris V, 1985).

[5] As Choplin put it, I think that mosques and commercial activities are the main constituents of public space in Nouakchott. See Choplin, *Nouakchott au carrefour de la Mauritanie et du monde* (Clamecy: Karthalla-Prodig, 2009), 161.

of 1 kilometer each, making an inventory along each of them to identify points of mobile phone purchase, their types, and the category of audio advertising they operate.

Moreover, I joined regular shuttles on the major public transportation routes as a way to evaluate the various audio equipment in taxis and the ways passengers reacted to the materiel selected. I also diversified my places of worship to observe a large number of mosques in a large number of districts. In addition, I balanced my time watching local channels and listening to FM radio broadcasts to get a wide overview of the programs carried.

The inquiry also involved recording many interviews with various actors and authorities. I recorded interviews with more than 10 taxi drivers, 20 mobile phone prepaid card sellers, 4 imams of mosques, 5 music shop owners, 3 merchants, 3 researchers, 2 broadcasting directors in public and private media, and the secretary general of the National Olympic Committee.

This article will, first, describe several expressions of religiosity that I have chronicled as they appear in the public space of this city and offer some comparisons of each, both diachronically and synchronically. In the second part it will provide an analysis of possible origins of these aspects of religiosity within the Moorish community of Nouakchott.

### *Religiosity in Public Space: Today and Yesterday*

Before delving into the city's religious landscape, it may be helpful to introduce a little of Nouakchott's history. The history of modern Nouakchott begins in 1903, when the French constructed a military camp around the ancient village of Ksar. This ultimately became the site of the current Mauritanian capital on July 24, 1957, when the construction of the city began. A modern center, called *Kapital*, appeared on the west side of the ancient nucleus, Ksar. After independence in 1960, Nouakchott continued to expand, but the greatest change occurred in 1972–73. During that period new quarters were founded alongside the original settlements of Ksar and *Kapital* (Tevragh Zayna): Sebkha and El-Mina on the south side and Teyaret on the north. More administrative districts were added in 1990 when the city reached a population of 500,000. These districts included Riyad, Arafat, and Dar Naim. In the meanwhile, Toujounine was created on the eastern side.

In this city, religion is of paramount importance and is easily observed in markers such as mosques, the city's cell phone business, and the soundscape[6] of the town.

### *The Mosque and Its Attendance*

#### An Increase in Numbers and an Increased Audience

What strikes many observers about Nouakchott is the large number of mosques. Almost every block has its own mosque. To accommodate the city's grown population, in many places the public land that was originally set aside by urban planners as green areas or leisure spaces has been invaded by new mosques, the government having no ability to refuse the use of the land for worship. This illegal appropriation of public land has given rise to some legal cases and a debate among ulama.[7] Some mosques are built with temporary materials with limited space for worship. The grand, architecturally distinguished mosques that we associate with the urban spaces of North Africa in Tunis or Rabat, for example, are few and are mainly those built by foreign governments: Saudi Arabia, Morocco, and Qatar.

The first of these mosques, the Saoudian, is the Nouakchott *ǧāmiʾ*—a mosque where the Friday prayer is performed and transmitted by public radio and television. Tijaniyya brotherhood mosques are also regarded in high standing, as well as the mosques funded by rich personalities in Tevragh Zeina, the most prosperous area of Nouakchott.

According to the last survey[8] conducted by the Ministry of Islamic Affairs, there are 992 mosques in Nouakchott servicing almost 900,000 inhabitants.[9] The people of Nouakchott show a great predilection to at-

[6] As reference to the current study and this particular concept, see Charles Hirschkind, *The Ethical Soundscape: Cassette Sermons and Islamic Counterpublics* (New York: Columbia University Press, 2006). The approach of this book is, however, different from mine given that Hirschkind addresses "the formation of sensorium," the acoustic aspects, the evaluation and impacts of performances among the public. In this paper it is rather a matter of the meaning of religious words and their commercial functions.

[7] Some scholars have argued that illegal space implicates illegal worshipping. Hamden Wuld Tah, a famous scholar of Nouakchott, blames people who use this as a means to get land, asserting that in doing so they arouse prejudice against Islam and Muslims.

[8] Islamic Republic of Mauritania, Ministry of Islamic Affairs and Original Teaching, *Report Summary of General Survey of Maḥaḍra and Mosque 2009/2010* (Nouakchott, July 2010).

[9] On the base of projection 879,000 in 2009, see the demographic table in Choplin, *Nouakchott*, 82.

tend the prayers at the mosques as opposed to other venues, such as their homes, and the audience often includes neighborhood children. Worship at home has become very uncommon. Even though some mosques have an area of worship set aside for women, their attendance at common prayers is quite rare. Nevertheless, the high concentration of mosques leads them to be less than full during the weekday prayers when only the first lines of the congregation are usually occupied.

The highest attendance occurs on Fridays when there is a rush to get to the mosque by 1:45 in the afternoon. People converge from all directions bringing their prayer carpets. Most mosques, regardless of their size or the educational level of their imam, are open to worshippers. Sometimes streets adjacent to the mosques are also full of participants. For the next hour the city remains calm, the only sound being loudspeakers dispensing the Friday sermons.

The month of Ramadan constitutes the other period of high attendance in the mosques. During this month, the *tarāwīh*, a supererogatory prayer that requires an average time of thirty minutes to complete, attracts many participants. The houses are almost empty during this night prayer and the city streets are nearly deserted. The number of women attending the mosques for *tarāwīh* also increases during this month.

In addition to mosques in residential areas, most institutions, companies, or administrative units of government have their own mosques. When the *muezzin* calls for the afternoon prayer at 2 PM, the employees leave their offices to go to the mosque. The prayer gathers institutional personnel as well as a few people from the surrounding area. The passersby attend the prayer, too, as well as passengers in passing cars. These "institutional mosques," although abandoned outside working hours, are well attended up to the sunset prayer. Located in general along the great avenues, people in traffic at this moment stop their cars and enter these mosques to pray. This image of Nouakchott center at this time of day is exemplified by the area in front of the Ministry of Education on Gamal Abdel Nasser Avenue, where great congestion is generally observed.

At the same time, huge crowds gather at the Madrid crossroad, at the junction of the three highways of Mauritania. There, passengers in taxis, buses, and cars constitute an ad hoc congregation. Passengers use the avenue sides to form prayer lines as they arrive at the crossroad. Eastward, Shifa Complex and Tenswaylim Mosque are overcrowded thanks to the users of the Boutilimit highway.

Many mosques broadcast by their loudspeakers audio recordings of the Qurʾan or sermons between the *adhan* and the beginning of prayer. During the usual prayer times, lines of worshippers in the mosques are few, as mentioned above, and worship is often followed by a talk on Islamic teachings, or a sermon on the topic of "prescribing the good and prohibiting evil." Such talks are mainly attended by the regular attendees of the mosque called *ǧamāʾit al-masǧid* (mosque community). This group, which represents the minimal attendance of the prayer, includes the imam, the muezzin, their respective assistants, and a few faithful from the neighborhood. It might also involve Qurʾanic students from Islamic traditional schools (*maḥaḍra*) usually attached to the mosque,[10] the imam generally being their teacher. It is particularly worthy to mention, however, the preponderance of youth attending prayers.

At the end of prayer a few events are announced, generally lectures presented by famous scholars in different Nouakchott mosques. The address and the time are provided to the audience. The performances of famous scholars as Wuld Sīdi Yaḥya[11] or Wuld Dedew[12] draw a great crowd to the designated mosque. Recently, one of the greatest Friday gatherings at a Nouakchott mosque occured in Tensouaylim, at the Dedew Mosque, when Wuld Dedew delivered his famous *Ruqya.*[13]

---

[10] According to the ministry, 559 mosques in Nouakchott have *maḥaḍra. See* Ministry of Islamic Affairs and Original Teaching, *Report Summary*, 23.

[11] Muḥammad Wuld Sīdi Yaḥya is an icon of Mauritanian Islamism and, since the 1980s, one of Nouakchott's most popular preachers (*duʾāt*). He was the first to bring religious teachings closer to the daily life of people. The distribution of his sermons through audio recordings created a real shift in access to Islamic knowledge, which was for centuries a hostage of the clerical class and obscure manuscripts. See Zekeria Ould Ahmed Salem, "Prêcher dans le désert: L'univers du Cheikh Sidi Yahya et l'évolution de l'Islamisme Mauritanien," *Islam et sociétés au sud du Sahara,* 14–15 (2000–2001): 13.

[12] Muḥammad al-Ḥasan Wuld Dedew is today the preeminent figure of Islamic learning in Mauritania. Wuld Dedew, who has a prodigious memory, was a strong presence in the prestigious *maḥaḍra* of his well-known family, Ahil ʿaddūd. He then became very famous among scholars of Arabic countries. In addition, his teaching in Middle East universities helped create a tremendous network among the Muslim scholars and politians across the Muslim world. He founded, in the Arafat area, an ulama training institute in the vicinity of his mosque. His cassettes, mainly dealing with technical matters of worship, are immensely popular, whereas his appearances on TV strengthen his notoriety in the larger Islamic world. Wuld Dedew is considered today the ideological touchstone of the *Tawāṣul* Party.

[13] *Ruqya* is a legal healing with specific verses from the Qurʾan. Hundreds of believers bring their water bottles or purchase them at the mosque, and after the prayer Wuld Dedew spits in those bottle. Once blessed throughout this act, everyone takes back his bottle.

One of the most amazing phenomena in the mosque universe is the relatively recent introduction of cell phones. Although every mosque posts signs requesting that mobile phones be turned off, people rarely silence them. As an alternative and to harmonize with the religious environment, individuals download Islamic phrases on their phones. As a result, it is common to hear various ring tones ranging from a muezzin call to Qurʾanic recitation, sermon excerpts, and religious exhortations during prayer.

## Modern and Classic Mosques

The contemporary situation in Nouakchott mosques contrasts with conduct in mosques before the arrival of new waves of Islamist influences in the 1970s.

Given the nomadic nature of traditional Moorish society, mosques as physical structures were very few in the period before 1970. Mungo Park, who visited eastern Mauritania in 1805, remarked that Moors "have no mosques . . . but perform their devotion in a sort of open shed, or enclosure made of mats."[14] More recently P. Dubié, quoted by H. T. Norris, presented *lamsīd* (local version of *masǧid*, the Arab word for "mosque") as "the open area demarcated for prayer" (Norris 1972, 28). In the Islamic classification, this kind of temporary worshipping place is called *muṣalla* and it was likely the most frequently used sacred space in nomadic life.

Within the confine of the *muṣalla*, all issues were debated, including profane ones, and humor was not absent. It was in fact a gathering space for relatives to pray but also to share before and after performing worship. Overall it was the informal nature of those spaces that was their major feature.

Mosques were an institution strictly tied to the sedentary regions. As a result, until recently most Mauritanians were not accustomed to gathering for communal prayer, worship being mostly an individual act due to the practical necessities of nomadic life.

The first mosque built in Nouakchott was that of Baddāh Wuld al-Buṣayrī in the Ksar constructed in 1958. In 1963 the Central Mosque was inaugurated in the eastern part of *Kapital*. A decade after independence the total number of mosques in Nouakchott still did not number ten, with a

---

[14] Mungo Park, *The Journal of a Mission to the Interior of Africa: In the year 1805* (London: printed for John Murray, 1815), 150.

preponderance of them affiliated with the Tijaniyya Sufi order.[15] Mauritanians of Pular descent, most of whom were followers of this mystical order, constituted a significant proportion of *Kapital*'s inhabitants by this time.

Through the 1970s, mosque attendance for communal prayer was rare. More typically the mosque served as a point of meeting for an imam's students and the followers of his Sufi order. The imam Baddāh Wuld al-Buṣayrī, in Ksar, and Muḥammad Ḥāmid, in the Medina, were mainly surrounded during the prayer by their disciples, both of them having a *maḥaḍra* in his mosque. Muḥammad ʿAbdallāh Wuld Daddāh reported that his father, who was a disciple of Muḥammad Ḥāmid, told him that in 1972 there were only a dozen who attended prayer regularly.[16] In the *Tijaniyya* mosques, attendance was limited almost exclusively to members of that Sufi order. In the list of his mosque group given to me, Thierno Daouda Ba cited only one person who did not belong to the *Tijaniyya.* It seems likely that the followers of this order erected mosques to reproduce what they were already familiar with in the urban region along the Senegal River and to maintain traditional ties between their communities.

In the 1960s and 1970s most Mauritanians with a nomadic background in Nouakchott performed prayers at home. In addition, it is plausible to speculate that some *zwāya* (scholar) families, numerous among civil servants and merchants of Nouakchott by this time, were reluctant to pray under the guidance of an imam they considered less qualified in Islamic sciences or representing a Sufi order different than their own. In the eastern *Kapital*, the *zwāya* houses always included a scholar or a guest coming from the countryside and deemed by the residents to possess sufficient Islamic knowledge to warrant appointment as their prayer leader. Having their own legitimate imam, they were exempted from going to a mosque whose imam was considered ignorant. For the common person, individual prayer was the rule and prayer was accomplished in private.

The presence of young men in the mosque was exceptional in the 1970s. Some traditions, even among the *zwāya*, indicated that it was not recommended for young people to be too firmly tied to worship.[17] This

[15] Interview with Thierno Daouda Ba, imam of îlot L Mosque founded in 1962, Nouakchott, August 20, 2012.

[16] Muḥammad ʿAbdallāh Wuld Daddāh, interview, October 23, 2011.

[17] This was suggested by Muḥammad Fall Wuld ʿAbd Al-Laṭīf in his recent autobiography; see Muhammad Fall Wuld ʿAbd Al-Laṭīf, *Al-Wālī al-Musāʾid* (Nouakchott: Dār al-Fikr, 2011), 182.

**Table 1. Number of mosques per inhabitant in Nouakchott**

| Year | Population | Mosques | Ratios mosques/inhabitants |
|---|---|---|---|
| 1962 | 5,807 | 2 | 2,903.50 |
| 1972 | 55,000 | 8 | 6,875.00 |
| 1989 | 620,000[a] | 46[b] | 13,478.26 |
| 2002 | 633,871 | 617[c] | 1,027.34 |
| 2005 | 743,511 | 730 | 1,018.50 |
| 2009 | 879,643 | 992[d] | 886.73 |

Source: Ould Ahmed Salem (2007) and Choplin (2009)

[a] Projections of the 1988 census applying annual growth rate of 5 percent. Besides, one should note that deportation of Senegalese and black Mauritanians had affected the city's population growth after 1989.

[b] See Zekeria Ould Ahmed Salem, "Islam in Mauritania, between Political Expansion and Globalization: Elites, Institutions, Knowledge, and Networks," in *Islam and Muslim Politics in Africa*, ed. Benjamin Soares and René Otayek (New York: Palgrave Macmillan, 2007), 40.

[c] Ibid.

[d] See Ministry of Islamic Affairs and Original Teaching, *Report Summary.*

would presumably protect them from psychological troubles, as an overdose of religiosity was believed to disturb the mind and lead to mental problems. Other activities such as going to the cinema were encouraged and became a widespread habit among young people at this time.

As table 1 above shows, the number of mosques in Nouakchott began to rise in the late 1980s, but the real shift occurred in the following decade, reaching its peak at the turn of the second millennium with a rate of one mosque per less than one thousand people.

This unprecedented increase piqued the interest of Ould Bara,[18] who conducted the first inquiry into the topic of mosque attendance in August 2002.[19] He focused on possible reasons for this rapid expansion, consider-

[18] This survey has constituted the core of his presentation: Yahya Ould Bara, "*L'Islam en ville: Réseaux de solidarité, réseaux politiques*" (paper presented at IRD workshop, "*La ville ou l'etat,*" Rouen, 2003). On the other hand, it has been largely used in Ould Ahmed Salem, "Islam in Mauritania." The author also commented on his main findings in this survey during an interview I conducted with him on September 1, 2012, in Nouakchott.

[19] Interview, September 1, 2012, Nouakchott.

ing the urban way of life, new funding sources, and government support. Furthermore, he tried to understand why the status of imam was coveted, given that more than 50 percent of them were disputed.

Among his findings, he noted that 62 percent of Nouakchott mosques were built thanks to funds from the Arab Gulf, although according to the League of Imams of Mauritania, this rate was only 40 percent.[20] On the other hand, according to my observations, the role of local donators should not be neglected.

Ould Bara also established a typology based on the ideological orientation of the mosque. Factors in this classification included the nature of the sermons, the background of the imam, and the identity of those who regularly attended prayers. Among Nouakchott mosques, Ould Bara held that 36 percent belonged to the *Tawāṣul* party, 25 percent to the *Tijaniyya* order, 17 percent to the *Tablīġi* group, and 15 percent to Salafists. But only twelve mosques in Nouakchott constituted focal points that attracted people from all quarters of the town. The most logical explanation for this was the ideology of these mosques. Overall Ould Bara concluded that Gulf money in the form of *zakat*[21] could explain the massive mosque building rate. However, mosques also collect incomes from the protective and curative activities of their imams.

Data published by the Ministry of Islamic Affairs strengthen Ould Bara's findings. According to this document, half of Mauritanian mosques have been built in the last decade.[22] The government contribution to mosque construction is nearly negligible, with official documents indicating only 3.3 percent of all mosques were erected using state funds prior to 2009.[23] The ministry also noted that 606 imams were supported by unidentified or undisclosed incomes.[24]

In this respect we should also highlight the close links between the mosques and commerce. The greatest mosques, such as the *Sebkha* Mosque, are generally surrounded by shops, the rents of which help fund them. The Moroccan Mosque remained almost hidden for twenty years until the demolition of the shops surrounding it in April 2008. Those who advocate the link between Islamic worship and commerce remind us that the Prophet Muḥammad was a merchant in his youth, and Moorish traditions value the blessed character of this activity; according to a popular adage,

[20] See Ould Ahmed Salem, "Islam in Mauritania," 40.

[21] Charitable donations.

[22] See Ministry of Islamic Affairs and Original Teaching, *Report Summary*, 10.

[23] Ibid., 12.

[24] Ibid., 17.

99 percent of opportunities to earn income reside in trade, mainly practiced by the *zwāya* group. Nevertheless it remains a profane activity and represents one of the numerous coexistences of forms of the profane and the sacred alongside each other in Nouakchott's religious space.

Along with the increase in the number of mosques came changes in ritual behavior. Parents began bringing their children to the mosque and new gestural attitudes such as crossing hands on one's chest made their appearance. Simultaneously, in most cases, the mosque's atmosphere became more rigorous; no one, for instance, was now allowed to exhibit Sufi behaviors such as the loud recitation of their litanies (*ḏikr*). All these practices, most likely imports from the Middle East, were tied to the ideology of scriptural reform.

The initial introduction of these practices can be traced to the late 1970s among a nucleus[25] of students and followers of Imam Baddāh Wuld al-Buṣayrī. This group gained notoriety through its infiltration of the official media, the unofficial support of activists in the Muslim League, and the benevolence of Baddāh Wuld al-Buṣayrī himself.[26] The group was largely limited to an elite stratum until the popular *da'wa* movement, which reached its height in the 1980s, as Ould Ahmed Salem has described:

> In the second half of the 1980s, preachers (*du'āt*) intensified their efforts at the level of everyday society and the *Tablighi Jama'a* was again tolerated because of its conspicuously apolitical character. It was even able to establish two preaching centers in the poorer neighborhoods of Nouakchott, all the while being officially supported by the major theologians and imams of the country. In fact, although its political influence had virtually disappeared, Islamism in Mauritania apparently redeployed itself in *da'wa* or the call to Islam. This "retreat" from politics allowed it to gain ground and to win acceptance and understanding from its immediate rivals, the ulama. In any case, it was through preaching in the mosques that the Islamist movement regained its vigor. It recruited in all the most vulnerable sectors of society, for example among Hara-

[25] In a recent paper, one of the founders of this movement presented an account of the first steps of the Islamist organization in Mauritania; see www.ak-akhbar.info, archives, November 28, 2010.

[26] The emergence of this movement is developed in Abdel Nasser Ould Ethmane Sid Ahmed Yessa, "L'opposition politique en Mauritanie: Discours et mode d'action depuis 1980" (Mémoire de maîtrise, Université de Nouakchott, 1987).

tines (former slaves or descendants of slaves), where it made spectacular inroads.[27]

One of the mosques mentioned here as being in the poorer neighborhoods of Nouakchott, the so-called preachers' mosque (*masğid al-duʾāt*), is located in Riyad, a mainly Haratines quarter. The location of this center, one of the largest, is therefore highly significant, and all observers have acknowledged the popularity of *daʾwa* among this social group.

The wide adherence of Haratines to the *daʾwa* is a symbolic act of emancipation; it is especially relevant that in their discourse they always refer to the Prophet Muḥammed's Companions, who mostly came from the lower social classes. The Haratines' support of the *daʾwa* movement is heavily indebted to the intensive activity of one major preacher-performer, Wuld Sīdi Yaḥya.

Ould Ahmed Salem has detailed Wuld Sīdi Yaḥya's speech, strategies, and techniques. He has particularly emphasized that his objective was to target this group with numerous references to a theology of poverty in his sermons.[28] He deals mostly with how rich people have the religious duty to help in addressing poverty and assisting their poor brothers.

The outcome of the increase of *daʾwa* among Haratines obviously contributed to intensify their numbers in mosques as well as their sympathy for Islamist ideas. Other nonclerical social groups joined the *daʾwa*, and elders became disturbed by the intrusion of both Islamists and Haratines into the mosques. Ultimately, incidents became frequent in the mosques where debates between traditional scholars and Islamists occasionally led to open clashes. On top of this, the Islamists' rejection of Sufism deepened the gap separating adherents from their elders, opening a divide that resembled a generational conflict. Elders became more and more reluctant to confront the growing number of "young rebels." However, a dozen mosques in Nouakchott remained in the control of what we may call "the classical standards." They are in general managed by a group of senior ulama led by recognized scholars of the *zwāya* tradition who allow all kinds of speech except for that of the Islamists. Their atmosphere is so relaxed that one might think he is in a social gathering. Those mosques are located mainly in Toujounine and Teyaret districts and are classified by Ould Bara as "tribal mosques." They represent the old fashion in nomadic society and their resistance to Islamism reveals a form of social class struggle and identity conflict.

---

[27] See Ould Ahmed Salem, "Islam in Mauritania," 30.

[28] Ould Ahmed Salem, "Prêcher dans le désert," 23.

This group of mosques received a significant boost when the Mauritanian government, claiming an Islamic plot in 2003, began to exert systematic control over imams and began a campaign to monitor sermons. Officials warned against those who disseminated "subversive messages"[29] which might be "foreign to the Islamic traditions of the country."[30] The state media focused at this time on the superfluous nature of importing Islamic ideas given "that Mauritanian scholars have always diffused Islam across the world."[31] This opinion was backed by some traditional scholars despite the fact that the country was deeply concerned by the government's oppression of imams. On the other hand, traditional scholars started to become more and more involved in the political scene and in the media. They began to feature in audiocassette productions of Islamic teachings and on cassettes about Mauritania's literary heritage. This trend was obviously strongly encouraged by the government, hoping that these repositories of the classical Islamic tradition of Bidan society could help counter the influence of Islamists.

Overall, government repression resulted in a shift in mosque activity: the *duʾāt* role steadily decreased and aspects of religiosity, in general, were impacted to varying degrees.

However, with this decline of *daʾwa* came a rise in the number of political activists, involving more non-Haratines members as well as the bankrupt political parties of the nationalists and Marxists. The emergence of this new wave of Islamism also found a favorable context in the liberalism of domestic policy, the explosion of Islamic TV satellite channels, the activism of Islamic institutions based in Nouakchott, and the role of the Mauritanian diaspora in the Arab Gulf.[32]

## *Mobile Phones*

### Shouting Sellers and Sacred Phrases

Among the soundscape of Nouakchott, shouting mobile phone sellers are the most salient. Loudspeakers advertise prepaid mobile phone cards or mobile phone accounts in most busy streets. Sellers often shout slogans

---

[29] See Ould Ahmed Salem, "Islam in Mauritania," 31.

[30] See *Horizons* 3470 (2003): 1.

[31] Ibid.

[32] See further details in Ould Ahmed Salem, "Islam in Mauritania," 30–39.

themselves, but all this commercial activity relies on a marketing strategy centered on Islamic messages. Proposals for phone service and prepaid mobile phone cards alternate with religious blessings and litanies.

Among the most frequent phrases are "*Bismiallāh al-Raḥmān al-raḥīm*" (In the name of Allah, the Most Gracious, the Most Merciful) or "*Assalāmu ʿalaykum wa raḥmatu Allāh*" (May the peace and the Mercy of Allah be upon you). These are followed by the types and prices of services and then the phrases are repeated. Interspersed more randomly are cries of "*Lā ilāha illa Allāh*" (There is no God worthy of worship except God) coupled with "*Muḥammad Rasūl Allāh*" (Muḥammad is the messenger of God). Other phrases are "*Lā Ḥawla wa lāquwwata illa bi- Allāh*" (There is no power nor strength other than the thanks of God) or more commonly "*Astaġfiru Allāh*" (May God forgive me).

Mobile phones appeared in Nouakchott in the year 2000. Their increase in use since that date is unparalleled by any economic activity the city has ever known. The returns earned by cell phone providers are tremendous and there have been moments when the mobile phone business seems to be the sole economic activity of Nouakchott.

Since 2000, three licenses have been allocated by the government to cell phone companies. The first operator to obtain a license was Mattel SA in 2000, followed by Mauritel SA in 2001 and Chinguitel SA in 2007. In all, these companies held 2,009,762 subscriptions in 2008 according to the Mauritanian Telecommunications Regulation Authority.[33] Given that the total Mauritanian population is estimated at 3,000,000, it is possible to conclude that Mauritania has more cell phones than adult inhabitants; in fact, most individuals have at least two subscriptions.

In short, the mobile phone today has invaded all fields of social interaction and its incredible success is due to the penchant of Mauritanians for gossip[34] and the spreading of rumors,[35] in which cell phones play a major role

[33] See Wane Saidou, "Usages du téléphone moblile et changements sociaux chez les Imraguin du banc d'Arguin, cas de Mamghar (Mauritanie)" (Master dissertation, Université Paris Descartes, Paris, 2009).

[34] It is very significant that every member of most family has at least two phones and that young people spend most of their time in calling each other. Even the poorest families dedicate a great part of their budgets to purchasing prepaid phone cards.

[35] Some observers interpret the multiplicity of newspapers (more than 700 receipts, or official documents making it legal to work in the journalism field), radio stations, and websites as indicators of the power of the rumor and its use as a mean of information in Mauritania. Ould Mahfoudh asserted that this phenomenon is so strong in Mauritania that it deserves

as they move across the city. An additional explanation comes in an eminent characteristic of Moorish behavior: a desire to acquire information,[36] which has played an important role in feeding the rapid growth of mobile phone consumption. This development needs to be seen alongside the marketing of sacred phrases. The unprecedented success of this business has reinforced strongly religious expressions in the public space which is permeated by Islamic resonances of all forms. We have already noted that ring tones use recorded Islamic expressions to match the trend toward great expression of religiosity, particularly within mosques and other public areas. It is highly symbolic that the headquarters of the most important mobile phone market in Nouakchott faces the biggest mosque in Nouakchott, the Saudi.

## New Technologies and Old Practice

The use of litanies and religious formulas in phone marketing were, in fact employed by Mauritanian entrepreneurs prior to the cell phone era. The first person to introduce such phrases to the Nouakchott soundscape was the notebook seller Sīdi Muḥammad wuld Ebbe, a self-made man who is an entrepreneurial success story.[37] In the mid-1990s I had observed him hailing people with "*kil shi ib miyya*" (everything costs 100) in the street running along the eastern side of Al-Mina Market. Later, I noted that he had added Islamic phrases to his pitch and finally he added a tape recorder,

its own science, which he called *rumeurologie* (French etymology) or *aswaqology* (for the Hassanyan etymology). See Habib Ould Mahfoudh, "Mauritanides," *Mauritanie Demain* 19 (1991): 4. The impact of rumor can occasionally be observed in real time. Last year, rumors about the injury of the president resulted in the saturation of cell phone lines for many hours and the virtual immobilization of the system.

[36] The collection of information can be viewed as a cultural and social legacy of the not so distant past. The Moors, as heirs of nomads, appreciate the vital need for information because it is necessary to know the road and the location of water in the desert. As such, the seemingly random accumulation of data is deemed a critical survival skill, since one never knows when such information may come in handy. To illustrate the lengths to which Mauritanians will go to collect information, one should remember the coup of June 2003, when inhabitants of Nouakchott stayed on rooftops throughout the fighting, braving tank shells, mortars, and stray bullets to see what was going on and then have the opportunity to narrate it.

[37] Sīdi Muḥammad, whose nickname in Nouakchott is Sīdi Muḥammad *Wantayr* (vendor), started his little stall with less than $200 in 1994. From selling notebooks in units he sold them later on in carton boxes. He introduced little by little other products and his trade was so prosperous that by 2000 his annual turnover reached $20,000 (interview, August 22, 2012).

dispensing the same litanies and advertisements as his business became increasingly prosperous. He then moved to a larger shop and began the use of a loudspeaker to diffuse his advertisements.

When I met him,[38] Sīdi Muḥammad told me that, at the time he opened this little stall in 1994, the first microphones and loudspeakers were just appearing on the market. He started using them to attract consumers who were impressed by this new device. In answer to my question about his introduction of the Islamic phrases, he told me that when he was repeating his leitmotif "*kilshi ib miyya*" many people told him "you should invoke your Lord, are you not afraid to die while repeating those evil words?"[39]

In fact, Islamic phrases belong to what is called chat expiation (*takfīr al-mağlis*). Its Islamic reference is in the following *hadith* reported by Abū Huraryra:

> The Prophet Muḥammad said those who sat over chatting or lying in a gathering and who said before he leaves this council: Glory to you my Lord and Praise be to you I bear witness that there is no God but you, I ask your forgiveness and I repent to you asking forgiveness for the sin that was in this gathering.[40]

These phrases are the usual ones, but any other religious phrase can serve as a stand-in to shift from profane speech and to remind one of who is his Lord and what is his religious duty; in doing so they become an expiation.

The success of Sīdi Muḥammad's business introduced the widespread use of loudspeaker advertisements using religious phrases across Nouakchott. Many merchants adopted the religious advertisement system of Sīdi Muḥammad *Wantayr* (vendor) as the practice spread steadily. When mobile phones were introduced in the early 2000s, this practice had become so strongly established and successful that vendors applied it immediately to announce their new products. Many mobile phone sellers believe such

[38] It took several months to meet Sīdi Muḥammad as he maintains a very nomadic trading style. He was often out of Nouakchott to sell products in the four corners of the country. I met him finally in a short stay between two trips and was introduced by a colleague of his. The interview took place at the home of this student, Wuld Barwaygat, in Teyaret. Interview, August 22, 2012.

[39] For Muslims, the best death is one during which the dying person repeats the confession of faith. In general, his relatives pronounce those phrases to help him in repeating them.

[40] M. A. M. al-Šawkānī, *Tuḥfat al-Ḏākirīn* (Beirut: Dār al-Našr, 1984, no. 1/270). Link at http://islamport.com/d/1/akh/1/73/505.html.

phrases bring good fortune to their trade. Furthermore, one cannot broadcast advertisements without introducing these phrases which, beyond their blessings and expiation, help attract customers.

In fact, when we examine this process, it appears to be a combination of good marketing, a definitely profane activity, and its religious antidote (the phrase *takfīr al-mağlis* is a pious term presumably used to clear the sin of chatting). This cohabitation of ideas seems to be characteristic of other aspects of religiosity in Nouakchott as it is for the soundscape in general.

### *Music Shops, Taxis, and Audiovisual Media*

#### The Religious Seal

Shops in Nouakchott dedicated to profane music contribute paradoxically to the Islamic orientation of the city. While dealing mainly in nonreligious entertainment, these establishments broadcast mainly religious material such as Qurʾanic readings, sermons, preaching, and Islamic teachings from their louspeakers on the street. Such materials, which had been a monopoly of a few religious bookshops (*maktaba islāmiyya*), are today common in all music shops locally nicknamed "*standard*."[41] Mostly located around markets, standards bombard the city with their high-decibel announcements of their products. The most popular standards are those of Clinic Street and Charles de Gaulle Avenue in *Kapital,* and in Al-Mina quarter, where they are concentrated adjacent to the taxi station on the east side of the market.

Among their sales, standards provide audiocassettes of religious litanies and phrases and phone advertisements from local mobile phone sellers. They also supply the mosques with the audios that are played before worship. Likewise, it is in those very shops that drivers get the audios played in taxis and buses.

Taxis in Nouakchott are regulated as public transportation and accept four to five passengers. Every taxi has its own tape recorder emitting similar kinds of Islamic audio material. During the whole trip, consumers are exposed to recitations of Qurʾanic verse or sermons. Sometimes a controversy arises regarding the choice of material, but the most frequently used cassettes are those of sermons of Wuld Sīdi Yaḥya and Wuld Dedew. The

---

[41] This term appeared to designate these shops at their beginning in the late 1970s, but I have never found any explanation for this designation nor its relationship with selling audiocassettes.

creation in 2009 of a radio station dedicated to Qurʾanic readings helps in strengthening this trend. Instead of playing cassettes, taxi drivers just tune in Radio Qurʾran and everyone in the car remains quiet, apparently satisfied.

The media in Mauritania have followed the Islamization movement soundscape. Radio Qurʾan broadcasts, as its label implies, the Qurʾan but also exegesis and prophetic hadith and hagiography as well as Islamic teachings. Radio Qurʾan is therefore completely religious. On the other hand, public television and radio in Nouakchott devote more and more of their programming to religious topics.[42] During Ramadan all forms of secular broadcasts are preempted. Even Arabic soap operas are replaced by religious programs devoted to the Prophet Muḥammad, or the lives of his Companions, as well as great Muslim heroes and battles. The most popular show on public Mauritanian TV remains *al-Sahra al-Ramādāniya* (Ramadan Evening), which features a physician and a religious scholar answering questions about public health and religious concerns.

Following the liberalization of the media in January 2012,[43] the new stations now devote a great deal of their time to various kinds of religious programming. As private media emphasized the religiosity of their programming, public outlets were forced to increase the proportion of their lineups dedicated to these topics.[44] Public TV and radio introduced new religious programming to compete with the new private media. In some cases they simply broadcast the same shows promoted by the newcomers.[45] It is highly significant that this media liberalization gives rise to competition in religious production as a strategy to attract the largest audience. In this respect, Chinguit TV and Mauritanides Radio relied during their first months on sermons by Wuld Sīdi Yaḥya and praise songs of the Prophet (*madḥ*) in order to draw a large audience.

The *madḥ* is a popular music performed by the former slaves (Haratines) with very rudimentary instruments[46] and is a great success as a re-

[42] Muḥammad Taqiyouallah Ladham, broadcasting manager at TVM (Public National Television), said that this approach appeared in the early 1990s and that it was a response to the feedback and requests of listeners and viewers. The public media then introduced more religious programs in response; interview, August 30, 2012.

[43] The first private licenses had been allocated in November 2011 by the Mauritanian High Authority for Press and Broadcasting, but tests would not start before February 2012.

[44] Muḫtār wuld Tammīn, director of Mauritanides Radio, interview, September 4, 2012.

[45] Muḥammad Taqiyouallah Ladham, interview, August 30, 2012.

[46] In general, *madḥ* in Mauritania utilizes drums, rhythmic clapping along with a lead singer occasionally accompanied by a flute, and more recently the guitar has also been introduced.

ligious genre of music. The words of *madḥ* are mainly tied to hagiographies of the Prophet Muḥammad and those of his close Companions and family members, especially his daughter Fatima. Sometimes these deal with Islamic ideals or God's attributes although in a very few cases, one can observe a secular subject within a *madḥ* recital. Nevertheless, *madḥ* is generally perceived as a pious activity aimed at worship and requests for forgiveness, given that the Prophet Muḥammad is the intercessor for Muslims with God, and his praise calls for God's forgiveness.

It was the private media that premiered significant programming devoted to *madḥ.* The public media responded by broadcasting this form of music more frequently. This genre is so popular that every year a sort of "*madḥ* academy" is organized by the Mauritanian public TV to select the best *maddāḥ* (singer). This successful show has, in turn, strengthened the popularity of *madḥ,* which has become a veritable social phenomenon in Nouakchott. The participants in the competition become celebrities, who appear frequently on other television shows and as featured performers in concerts devoted to traditional music. Traditional musicians record in duos with *maddāḥ* and some have begun to introduce *madḥ* into their performances. In addition, Nouakchott wedding ceremonies have now added *madḥ* recitals to their classical musical repertoire.

*Madḥ* is also included in music shops along with other Islamic genres, but the most striking fact is what we observe at increasingly popular Nouakchott picnics. This new pastime that attracts people to the city limits, where they enjoy wilderness sands, inevitably includes a *madḥ* performance for the amusement of the picnickers. Some groups engage professionals while others employ amateur *maddāḥ*. But the great irony is that *madḥ* was a constituent of traditional nomadic life, momentarily lost with urbanization. Thanks to the media and the religious demand today, it has been rehabilitated and is enjoying a renaissance of a sort among urbane picnickers seeking a day in the country. *Madḥ* fever is currently proliferating toward other Mauritanian cities. Atar, in the center of the country, now has its own *madḥ* festival and Zouerate, in the extreme north, organized its first *madḥ* carnival in 2012.

## Sacred Time

As mentioned previously, what we hear today in the Nouakchott streets, on radio and tape recorders, when riding taxis and buses is mainly a mixture of Islamic axioms, Qurʾanic recitations, sermons, and so on. This provides an Islamic brand to the soundscape, but it is also a commercial strategy and a communicative policy.

The music shops play these because they sell them and they are therefore a part of their marketing. Furthermore, when I talked with shopkeepers, they told me that their advertising program is a result of compromise with their neighbors. Music shop owners were in the past the object of many complaints. They have often been summoned to police stations and threatened with legal action for the noises coming from their shops. Finally, they signed agreements, accepted by the major music sellers associations, whereby a shop will follow a precise timetable for broadcasting samples of their wares with particular reference to the daily prayer schedule. Only Qurʾanic recitation, sermons and the like can be broadcast during prayer times.[47] Some music shops respect this timetable and advertise their nonreligious music at other hours, but many of them elect to broadcast religious elements although they sell mostly secular music. This tends to undermine the previously prosperous Islamic audio shops (*al-maktabāt al-islāmiya*), the biggest of which, located on Gamal Abdel Nasser Avenue, went bankrupt, and the sales of others, formerly major outlets such as al-Quds on the *Kapital* central are, at this writing, steadily decreasing.[48]

Public recognition of sacred time also enters into public radio programming. In the early days of Nouakchott, broadcasting Qurʾanic recitations at the beginning of the programs was the preeminent indication of sacred time. But the program schedule had profoundly changed by the beginning of 1990s. In 1992, a self-consciously religious show called *Ramadāniyāt ʿalā al-Hawā* was put on the air. The same Ramadan show with *Al-Sahra al-Ramādāniya* was introduced on public TV in 1993.[49] Many other religious programs were added in the following years. The broadcasting manager of TVM asserts that his schedule is based on public opinion. Traditional scholars, in their reaction against Islamists, jumped on this unprecedented opportunity to share directly with the public. The religious elements have become more and more predominant in the broadcasting on public radio, which begins the day with Qurʾanic recitation and continues with religious programming thereafter. On Fridays and during Ramadan the programs remain strictly religious.

Nevertheless, those religious programs include musical and other

---

[47] SidʾAhmed Wuld Emmine, TOP Star standard owner, interview, August 27, 2012.

[48] Muḥammad, music shop owner, *Kapital* Market, interview, June 15, 2012.

[49] Muḥammad Taqiyouallah Ladham, interview, August 30, 2012.

lighter elements. The first of them is the widely diffused *madḥ,* we have already noted: a traditional religious music marinated in profane forms with the use of drums, flutes, and so on. In addition, recitations of religious poems are performed by scholars according to musical rules and modes. The most famous scholars in this respect are Wuld Maggāhi who sings Sufi poetry of his own creation; the second example is that of Amnāt Ashfaġa Aʾmar, famous for praise of the Prophet Muḥammad, accompanied by musical instruments. These programs, although their context and purposes are religious, afford often pleasant and delightful moments of entertainment which are not necessarily associated with piety.

Of course, another reason to broadcast religious elements is to keep a maximum audience entertained. In fact, social rules delimit topics that groups of different ages can share. In this context religious subjects are totally appropriate. There is an old adage in Moorish society that respects "things which do not disband the group" (*mā ifarrag ağmāʾa*). With respect to this, Wuld Tammīn, director of programming for Mauritanides Radio, said: "When we are to broadcast an interesting show, we try to keep the audience. We do not put on the air what could disperse our audience."[50] In the case of religious material, it is by definition an ideal medium since it is regarded as neutral, that is to say all ages could stay together and listen to it without any trouble.

This material is largely the same we hear in taxis and buses and which often follow the respect for "sacred time," namely listening only to religious materials at particular moments of the day. As we mentioned for music shops, taxi drivers tried at the beginning to apply this rule in order to satisfy customers' demands, or at least to avoid disputes among them. At daybreak and at nightfall, customers have no objections to any Islamic element; in fact, this meets with a form of unanimity. At other times, customers can request music and this can lead to disputes among passengers of diverse political or artistic persuasions. Amadou, a taxi driver in the Tevragh Zayna area, told me that he was often obliged to turn off the tape recorder as a result of such disputes.[51] Hasen, another taxi driver, on the Toujounine axis, tries to divine the customers' background on the basis of their dress and then chooses the appropriate broadcast.[52] Given the need to provide entertainment for consumers, many taxis broadcast Wuld Sīdi Yaḥya sermons. In fact the popularity of this preacher, we have already

[50] Mukhtar wuld Tammin, interview, September 4, 2012.

[51] Interview, May 21, 2012.

[52] Interview, July 27, 2012.

noted, is also founded on his humor[53] and populism. This component of his sermons is widely appreciated and affords a double purpose for those producing the broadcast: mixing the religious with a form of entertainment.

The significance of religious content is, therefore, chiefly a matter of timing. The holy times of the day are defined by the Qurʾan and Prophetic tradition. In the Qurʾan it is said: "And ask forgiveness of thy sin, and hymn the praise of thy Lord at fall of night and in the early hours" (*Ġāfir* 55) and "glorify His Praises, morning and afternoon" (*al-Aḥzāb* 41–42). The reference in hadith is the following:

> Abu Hurayrah, may Allah be pleased with him, said that the Messenger of Allah, peace be upon him said:
>
> "The angels took turns to dawn prayer and dusk prayer. The Omniscient Lord asks those who spent the night: 'how did you find my slaves?' and they respond 'they were praying when we came and we left them praying'"[54]

According to Islamic scriptures, the two moments of the day that should be dedicated to worship are sunrise and sunset. They constitute the ideal moment of adoration. In the *zwāya* tradition, these were the times that were completely devoted to the litanies and corresponded to a period of silence. If pressed, those who were obliged to talk did so only in Arabic, a sacred language that was appropriate to the sacred moment. Those are the times of meditation and contemplation when no other activity should disturb the soul of the believers. That, probably, is what the soundscape in Nouakchott reflects. In Mauritanides Radio, for instance, religious lectures are programmed from 7 to 8 AM, whereas Qurʾanic recitation is broadcast between 5 to 7 PM[55] Except during these intervals, other programs can take place.

## *Clothing*

### Islamic Labels

In Nouakchott streets, it is rare to meet women wearing the *niqāb,* those long black *ǧallāba* covering the whole body. This kind of garment seems

---

[53] Zakaria noted to this respect: "*Dans les prêches, l'intention comique se glisse absolument partout*"; Ould Ahmed Salem, "Prêcher dans le désert," 32.

[54] Al-Bukhari Collection.

[55] Wuld Tammīn, interview, September 4, 2012.

to be limited to very conservative groups, mostly descendants of Salafists, their relatives and acquaintances.

More frequently, one observes men in white *ǧallāba*, in various places and contexts. These *ǧallāba* could in some cases be in other colors; but the white clothes are a widely respected symbol of religiosity.

Adult males are generally bearded but the beards are very diverse. Among Islamists, hair is freely growing in order to get the thickest possible beard. Common people wear a less dense beard. The younger men usually have regularly shortened beards.

The use of the face veil (*liṯām*) is widespread among men of a mature age. The *liṯām* worn the *duʾāt* way is observed by some but not widespread. This characteristic *duʾāt* way is supposed to belong to the tradition of dressing by the Prophet Muḥammad. It consists of wrapping a veil around the head and leaving a part of it hanging upon neck and shoulders. The veils are in general made of white material. And white material is more and more frequently found in shops and stores. White garments imported from the Middle East have come into great demand, particularly the Saudi brand *Hantouch* based in Jedda that specializes in white clothing.

## Veiling the People of the Veil

Some elements of Islamic fashion coming from the Middle East made a timid appearance in Nouakchott side by side with the ideological influence of Islamism. Those phenomena remained, however, limited and the traditional garments—both the veil (*malaḥfa*) for women and gown (*darrāʾa*) for men—remain widespread. One must remember that Moorish society is broadly conservative and women's dress generally follows Islamic standards. The *malaḥfa* on which all the body is wrapped also covers the head and prevents Islamists' critiques that rely on uncovered hair (*sufūr*) as an argument in their propaganda. There have been campaigns against thin and transparent material for the veil in Nouakchott conducted by the ulama in recent decades. Although these campaigns were unsuccessful, it is noteworthy that scholars targeted the material but not the clothes and they have not called explicitly to ban the veil or to replace it with the *niqāb* or *burka* or any other Islamist garment.

Simard explains how the Moorish women's veil fits Islamic requirements while avoiding the full rigor of Islamist clothing:

> Sur le plan religieux, la *malahfa* répond aux exigences de l'Islam qui demandent à la femme de couvrir son corps décemment. Il faut mentionner que

> la *malahfa*, avec la variété de ses couleurs, se distingue nettement du tchador et du foulard musulman, caractérisés par leur rigueur et leur austérité.[56]
>
> On the religious level, the *malahfa* meets the obligations of Islam that require the woman to cover her body decently. It should be noted that the *malahfa*, with its variety of colors, is clearly distinct from the Muslim headscarf and chador, characterized by their rigor and austerity

The author then gives testimonies from two women in Nouakchott, comparing their clothes with the *tchador* and their respective religious functions, which are the same in their sense:

> La femme musulmane doit se couvrir, elle ne doit pas exposer son corps. Je ne porterais pas le tchador, non jamais. Le voile me suffit.
>
> La femme qui porte le tchador je la plains. Elle étouffe. Elle est peut être mieux vue que nous par l'Islam, mais, nous, on ne pense pas qu'elle est meilleure musulmane que nous. Ici, ce n'est pas par rapport aux autres qu'on croit, c'est par rapport à nous et à Dieu.[57]
>
> The Muslim woman must be well covered; she must not exhibit her body. I would never wear the chador, no never. The veil is enough for me.
>
> I pity the woman who wears the *niqab*. She chokes. She may appear to be a better Muslim than we are, but we, we do not think she is better than us. Here, the faith is not meant to people, it is rather a tie between us and God.

One should underline in this latter testimony the pride implicit in Moorish ideas of religiosity among members of this society that, they are convinced, is the font of "True Islam."

Another traditional behavior, that of gender separation and interdiction for men to handshake with women, also prevents Islamists from making one of their capital arguments within Moorish society.

Regarding male dress, the turban (*liṯām* or *ḥawli*) is common clothing which can be traced back to the Almoravid movement of the eleventh century and the "people of the veil" who populated the Sahara in the medieval era.

---

[56] G. Simard, *Petites commerçantes de Mauritanie, voiles, perles et henné* (Paris: Karthala, 2000), 119.

[57] Ibid.

Mungo Park noted in the late eighteenth century wrote that "they [the Moors] have all adapted that characteristic of the Mohamedan sect, the turban."[58]

Given that it is deeply rooted in Moorish tradition, the turban has not been disturbed by the waves of dressing fashion associated with Islamism. But although the Islamist turban did not engender a great number of followers, the new Islamic trend lies in the prominence of the color white in a context previously dominated by black.[59]

Similarly, Moors are a bearded people and the beard is one of the critical elements of their male facial aesthetic. Mungo Park's beard helped him during his captivity in a Moorish camp:

> Such of the Moors as have long beards, display them with a mixture of pride and satisfaction, as denoting an Arab ancestry . . . If any one circumstance excited among them favorable thoughts towards my own person, it was my beard; which was now grown at an enormous length, and was always beheld with approbation or envy.[60]

Beards, then, are not foreign in Mauritania and the call of Islamism to be bearded was welcomed among Moors who almost consider cutting a beard as a deviation from the *sunna.* In popular debates, beard abuse is often cited with alcohol drinking as one of the great sins.

### *Public Displays of Piety and Religiosity*

One of the last aspects of public marks of religiosity is the use of *tasbīḥ* (prayer beads/rosaries) in sports. During the first hours of the morning, people do their "slow jogging" to sustain a healthy lifestyle and particularly for medical purposes. People, generally of a certain age, hold in between their fingers rosaries that the body movement shakes back and forth. In the Olympic stadium and its vicinity one can observe the same activity particularly at the sunrise. In short, the city is experiencing a reemergence of rosaries as traditional Muslim equipment particularly tied to the Sufi orders, and they have become symbols of religious duty coupled with physical activity.

[58] Park, *The Journal of a Mission*, 154.

[59] The color black has an aesthetic role and was almost exclusively present in the market during past centuries.

[60] Park, *The Journal of a Mission*, 154.

We have already mentioned the use of phones in mosques where the sound of ring tones is nearly continuous, but the most striking thing is that either prior to prayer or after its fulfillment, it is very common in Nouakchott today to hear someone loudly answering in his cell phone "Oh! Right now, I am in the mosque." The purpose of such behavior is to vocally inform others that the person is attending prayer at mosque.

Another sign of religious exhibitionism is observed during the month of Ramadan. It is frequent that talk in family gatherings and among friends typically focuses on the imam's performances in memorizing and reciting the Qur'an,[61] the two biggest challenges for *tarāwīḥ* prayer competency. Every person of the assembly praises the performance of the imam of his mosque, saying usually: "if you don't perform *tarāwīḥ* with so and so you are wasting your time, his is without equal," and each respondent naturally supports his own imam and at the end of the conversation no one is generally convinced, but the speaker's credentials of having attended such-and-such a mosque are well established.

That behavior is not limited to Ramadan, and it has become more and more frequent that people talk about their attendance at mosque and their worship.

### *Contemporary Revivalist Influences or Local Emergences of Traditional Practices*

These aspects of religiosity in the public space of Nouakchott prompt us to ask what part of these activities is of external provenance, a result of the contemporary Islamic revival, and what part is but a modern version of something with roots in the traditional religiosity of Moorish society? In addition, what, if any, is the interconnection between these two factors? Each of the examples of contemporary religiosity noted above bears an imprint of both the influence of Islamism and centuries-old religiosity in Moorish society.

#### The Traditional Impact: A Compromise

The examples of traditional dress versus Islamist fashions may give the impression that Islamist propaganda in Nouakchott is "stating the obvious."

[61] The reading of the Qur'an (*tağwīd*) has rigorous rules that vary according to the various schools.

Those who support this assertion argue that the deep levels and local symbols of religiosity in Moorish society make the new waves of "proselytism" completely irrelevant.

This assertion may appear extreme, especially in light of the influence of worldwide streams of Islamism, but in assessing today's religious behavior in Nouakchott we find it strongly rooted in a traditional form of Islam experienced by Moorish society throughout its history.

The management of a sacred time in fact implies that there is room for a "profane" time, and overall one should note a continual attempt in these practices to combine religious obligations with what is also pleasant and useful, a combination which is not conceivable from a fundamentalist perspective. The numerous jobs we mentioned in the mobile phone business, in music, and the media have their Islamic brand that serves the dual function of supporting business and making them religiously acceptable. On the other hand, in the fields of music and media broadcasting, the piety of the element does not eliminate its effect as entertainment.

Surely, some ostentatious displays do exist, such as sporting rosaries, and making public claims to regular mosque attendance have no roots in the traditional practices of Moorish Islam. In fact, the traditional practices always reference a more discreet approach to worship. It is said that so and so has some ties with Allah (*baynu ši mʾa mulāna*). Worship and the faith are between the believer and his God. The general rule is to worship in a secluded spot. Another adage is significant in this respect, so to qualify a religious person it is often said: "*maʾlūma sarīrtu*" (he has a private well). Religiosity is therefore an internal truth and the more confidential it is, the stronger is the faith. The pious person avoids any showy behavior while performing their religious duty. This discretion is also a mark of humility linked to piety and contrasts deeply with conspicuous behavior.

This ethos contrasts with certain demonstrations of religiosity mentioned above and evaluations of worship performances such as those who talk about the competency of an imam's memory for *tarāwīḥ* prayer and/or the imam who cries during the prayer. Any form of ostentation in one's worship is reproved in Islam, and is blameworthy behavior, called *riyyā*. Such behavior can even raise questions about one's belief.

Some aspects of religiosity in Nouakchott today are therefore very far from the humble way of worshipping that the city experienced in its first decades and even further from the traditional practices of the Moorish society. This simple and modest practice of Islam was particularly characteristic of *zwāya* religious culture,[62] which cultivated an undemonstrative attitude and observance of their religion.

This is not to say that ostentation does not exist in Moorish traditions, but it is mainly associated with the *Banū Ḥassān* (warriors). In describing this, Lesourd evoked the ancient, and very ostentatious, honor competitions that took place between the *Banū Ḥassān* lineages (*fayš*).[63] But the traditional standard used here to evaluate the evolution of ideas about appropriate religious behaviors belongs in fact to the *zwāya* group and environment, which had a huge influence in forming urban notions of Islamic behavior in Nouakchott. That overwhelming role of the *zwāya* led some to refer to a process of "*maraboutisation*"[64] in modern Mauritania.

*Zwāya* values have been steadily adapted by Nouakchott Moorish inhabitants as a way of spiritual salvation, and they have become a social model in this respect. The religious practices and teachings that are the domain of this group are nowadays adopted by other social groups. All people send their children to Qurʾanic schools where they are taught by *zwāya*. Wealthy people in Nouakchott can afford to send their children to *maḥḍra* in the countryside for the classical Islamic tradition of Bidan society teachings. Since the 1990s, the greeting "*waḫayrt,*" previously used to address holy men (a Sufi shaykh or pious scholar), has been extended to regular greetings. On the other hand, the adherence to a populist Islamism, as we have seen for the Haratines, can be interpreted as another way that *zwāya* values and ideals have been sought by the shortest path, a kind of "fast food" in religious teachings provided by Islamists. We can therefore deduce that the introduction of Islamism has provoked interactions within and between the social hierarchy of Moorish

[62] This is a concept borrowed from Nouhi, who defined it as a culture "affixed to the *zwāya* as a social group, to refer to the beliefs and practices that made up the form of Islam specific to these scholarly elites and their community." See Nouhi, "Religion and Society in Saharan Tribes: Authority and Power in the Zawaya's Religious Culture" (Ph.D. diss., University of Alberta, 2009), 46.

[63] C. Lesourd, "Le mesrah: Regard sur la 'culture matérielle du succès' à Nouakchott," *L'Année du Maghreb* (online) 4 (October 2008): 7.

[64] This concept has been popularized by Habib Ould Mahfoudh, who depicted the emergence of the *zwāya* class since the colonial period and its strengthening with the independent state which erected the "*République maraboutique de Mauritanie.*" The parallel is generally seen with warriors (*Banū Ḥassān*) who were the previous holders of political power in the traditional society. See Habib Ould Mahfoudh, "Mauritanides," *Le Calame* 242 (1998): 4–5.

society. Adherence to an Islamism, or its denial, then takes the shape of identity struggle. In all these cases the *zwāya* practice remains the crucial norm or standard against which other forms of Islamic practice are measured.

## Clerical Groups and Islamism: The Atypical Case of Mauritania

To understand the role of the clerical (*zwāya*) groups in negotiating Islamism in Nouakchott, it is helpful to introduce some comparisons with the emergence and expansion of Islamism in the other cities of the Muslim world.

For the Egyptian case, one of the best studied and the base of the Muslim Brotherhood, Kepel explained at length the catastrophic situation in Egyptian universities (deficient infrastructure, lack of books, pitiful teachers' salaries, promiscuity, etc.) to point out that the *Ǧamāʾa islāmiya* (Egyptian Muslim Brotherhood) drew their considerable strength from their ability to identify [those problems] and "to propose immediate solutions."[65] Obviously, to get complete access to the accommodations afforded by the Islamists, students had to be members of the *Ǧamāʾa.* Within a favorable political context (the regime's objectives of weakening leftist parties), the Islamists became the real masters of the Cairo campus, organizing all kinds of activities ranging from sports to public sermons and mosque meetings. The campus stood as the laboratory for Cairo *jahiliya*[66] society transformations. This process then spread to other segments of Egyptian society, with the first step being to encourage students to bring their parents to mosque, and then the children of those latter, and so on,[67] the final objective being having the whole student family involved in the process.

This strategy is close to that used by Tunisian Islamists who targeted the schools and universities from which students turned to calling their parents to worship. In Tunis, "Islamist students of both urban and rural origin also frequently report that as a result of their own conviction, their parents have been persuaded to carry out more faithfully the Islamic rites of prayer and

[65] G. Kepel, *Muslim Extremism in Egypt: The Prophet and the Pharaoh*, trans. John Rothschild (Berkeley: University of California Press, 1986), 136.

[66] Concept used by Hasan al-Banna and referring to the polytheism of the Arabian Peninsula before the emergence of Islam; it stands for Egyptian society's decay and corruption in his opinion.

[67] Kepel, *Muslim Extremism in Egypt*, 142–46.

fasting."[68] Besides, the young men coming from the countryside benefited from the help of their Islamists classmates "and started to worship."[69]

In the Mauritanian case, at the beginning of the *da'wa*, when *du'āt* were mostly Pakistanis, they recruited their first followers among the unemployed and marginalized groups in the late 1970s. We can suspect that drought and the breakdown of traditional boundaries within their tribes made those people the most fragile fragment of the society. The first significant group was actually that of *Takusu* (unemployed center), the space where unemployed people waited for employers seeking temporary help and spent their time playing cards. This group made a spectacular eruption in the closest mosque. It has been reported an increasing number of *Takusu* members attending prayer in Muḥammad Ḥāmed mosque.[70]

The real extension of Islamism, however, took place in the 1980s with the prominent role of Muḥammad Wuld Sīdi Yaḥya and his attraction of massive numbers of Haratines. This group had the most modest education in Arabic and Islamic sciences and was therefore the most vulnerable to receive the *da'wa* teaching that they saw as a form of emancipation and a possible change in their social status. Other groups, such as the *Banū Ḥassān* and casted classes, also entered this movement which permitted them a religious status and role that traditional society refused them. The *zwāya*, of course, contributed to the expansion of Islamism in this stage of Nouakchott's Islamic revival, but their role was more political than religious as it would appear in the following waves of Islamism.

The elders, in general, engaged in a fierce struggle against the *du'āt*. This opposition was fed by many factors and was strong among *zwāya* who were the majority of the mosque community and who would maintain their monopoly by eliminating any opportunity for emancipation by other groups. Among those factors one can note the Sufi orientation of some shaykhs who were targeted by the Wahhabist orientation of *du'āt,* and the refusal of those scholars to become disciples of "ignorant outsiders." Overall, a generational struggle was preeminent and the multiplication of mosques can be partly explained by the litigation across generations.

The *du'āt* movement in Nouakchott, in short, exhibited the opposite of what happened in Cairo and Tunis: it did not target students but was rather oriented to the lower social classes who were not able to convey

---

[68] Susan Waltz, "Islamist Appeal in Tunisia," *North Africa* 40, no. 4 (Autumn 1986): 656.

[69] Ibid., 668

[70] Mohamed Abdellah Ould Deddah, interview, October 23, 2011.

the message with the required depth for social and political reasons. Their humble status hindered their propaganda value among other social groups. In addition, the government did not encourage the *da'wa,* which remained suspect up to the time of the wave of repression that befell Islamists in 2003.

Another difference between Nouakchott and the other two capital cities is that the social structures in Nouakchott were able to respond to individual needs, and internal tribal assistance is highly efficient. Even in the case of the Haratines, their recourse to make demands on the lineage structure to which they were once attached, in times of need, remains a constant in the suburban areas. It is worth noting in this regard that even spatial divisions in Nouakchott retain a certain form of regional and tribal division of space: the north (Teyaret, Ksar) is mainly inhabited by northerners, eastern areas such as Toujounine are mainly the domain of easterners, and so on.

The second wave of Islamists, above all political, was mainly supported by middle-class students, civil servants, and merchants, and was deeply tied to those traditional social structures. In both cases, Haratines and the second wave of Islamists, the matter of worship was never at issue since worship style is so deeply ingrained among Mauritanians. Although it is possible to say that an individual may be more frequently in the mosque, we can never say that a person starts praying as a result of his or her adherence to a movement. The major difference between Nouakchott and the Egyptian and Tunisian examples lies in this very absence of *jahiliyya* as espoused by al-Banna.[71]

## The Problems for Islamism in a Society Ignorant of Secularism

Egyptian society, as well as Tunisian, has been affected by deep transformations during the past two centuries with the introduction of capitalism and Western modernity in the era of European imperialism. The introduction of modern transportation, basic industrialization, print media, and judicial reforms were among the most salient means of this modernization, which also impacted the role and influence of religion in daily life. This evolution gave rise, particularly in Egypt, to a new stratum of urban population attracted by a Western-influenced way of life and distanced from its traditional society and, particularly, its religion. In Tunisia, Bourguibism

[71] See Kepel, *Muslim Extremism in Egypt*, 142–46.

tried to apply an Attaturk model consisting of a pragmatic modernization where the place of Islam was limited or sometimes banned.

This Westernization, coupled with decreasing religiosity, laid the foundation for an appeal to Islamic roots, especially in times of economic and social crisis.

In Mauritania, colonization as a major means of modernization was only a brief period (a half century), and its influence did not go beyond the sedentary region of the Senegal River. The majority of the country was a nomadic space nicknamed by the French as the *vide* (vacuum) and was largely ignored. One result was that religion was not submitted to the erosive effects of colonization, and there was little effect upon religiosity and consequently no parallel to the appeal of Islamism as it appeared in Cairo or Tunis.

The struggle today in both Egypt and Tunisia is between secularists and Islamists. It is striking to note that the Islamists of today are strongly established where secularism reached its peak, thus triggering the appeal of Islam (Turkey, Tunisia, Egypt). In Iran, secularism gave us the Islamist revolution and the reign of mullahs.

In Mauritania, where secularism never had an opportunity to catch on, the struggle introduced by the Islamists is between themselves and traditional scholars; in consequence, the several waves of Islamism in post-independent Mauritania have been relatively weak. The *Tawāṣul* Party, despite its dynamism and its real success among the workers and student unions, has only 73,485[72] members in an electoral college that numbered 1,265,063 in 2009.[73]

The tribal system is still the strongest social structure in Mauritania, and the traditional clerical class remains very influential in the religious field. On the other hand, the government relies on this class in its struggle to counter the Islamists. When the first dialogue between Islamists and the government started in January 2008, the ulama directed the negotiations and, as a result, dozens of Islamists gave up extremism, announcing their rejection of violence. The ulama of the countryside are the sole local institutions to face an Islamist ideology, and this is done with the very effective weapon of Islamic scriptures and interpretations. The actions of

[72] Official party statistics. See also Jamil Mansour's speech at the second National Congress of the party in December 2012.

[73] Presidential Election Proclamation of the results of the presidential election of July 18, 2009, Constitutional Court, July 23, 2009. At the elections Jamil Mansour, the *Tawaṣul* Party leader, got 4.74 percent of the voices. See the same proclamation.

the traditional scholars take place either in private, at a personal level, or through public forums monitored by the government.

The other trait of classical Islamic tradition within Bidan society is its relative moderation and tolerance compared to the general tenure of the radical Islamists who seek to implement rigorous lifestyles with severe rules bordering on asceticism. The Moorish traditional scholars (who were nurtured on their own, nomadic version of asceticism) by contrast have a tradition of great tolerance. It is likely that the form of cohabitation between the sacred and profane depicted above is mostly the outcome of a negotiating process. In each aspect of the "new" religiosity in Nouakchott, we have seen a compromise that cannot be accepted within a strict Islamist view. The tradition of the *zwāya* combines piety, knowledge, and a certain philosophy of life which does not prohibit the pleasant aspects of the world. One of their meaningful maxims in this respect is that "given that life is a [long] voyage, it is then permissible to make it amusing" (*al-danya safar wa alʾabaṯ fʾas-safar mandūb*). It is noteworthy that *mandūb,* conveyed here by the word "permissible," is one of the steps in the scale of licit acts in Islam. In fact, making life's journey pleasant is not only tolerated but recommended. Furthermore, a very popular line of a poem[74] often cited in this context asserts that the ideal person is he who combines worship with distraction, encapsulated in a famous Moorish maxim: *Sāʾa li-Allāhi u sāʾa l-i al-malāhi* ([There is] a time for God and a time for entertainment).

It has been mentioned above how the playful atmosphere one encounters in a mosque is a characteristic of ancient practice. The most popular jokes in the oral heritage of Moors belong to the *zwāya* tribes, particularly Awlad Dayman, Idayqib, and Idab Lihsan, three tribes especially venerated for their religious scholarship. It is relevant to note, in this respect, that the Awlad Dayman and Idayqib had a significant presence in Nouakchott during the first decades of its foundation. They were both in the administration and were liberally found among the merchants both in their homeland and the adjacent regions, as were also members of the Idab Lihsan.

This moderating attitude of the *zwāya* may also be explained as the outcome of their cohabitation with *Banū Ḥassān*. The long span of time, at

---

[74] The verse is :

*Falillāhi minnī ğānibun lā uḍīʾuhū* *wa li—allahwi minnī wa al-biṭālati ğānibu*
(a part of my time is dedicated to Allah; amusement and comfort get the other side)

least three centuries, during which the *Banū Ḥassān* held political power alongside the *zwāya* who were devoted to religious and intellectual pursuits, may have tamed the zealous Islam of the *zwāya*, drawing them to a rather moderate form. Has the *modus vivendi* between the *Banū Ḥassān* defenders of secular values and the *zwāya* custodians of spiritual values impacted contemporary forms of religiosity which are a sort of median solution? Whatever is the legitimacy of this interpretation, or its operationality, the *zwāya* values that confront advocates of Islamism are broadly liberal and encompass local realities.

## *Conclusion*

Inspired by the ulama, who are products of Bidan society's classical Islamic tradition, Nouakchott society has embraced the influences of Islamism in mitigated forms that have left room for some entertainment and enjoyment. On the other hand, the ulama have provided intellectual skills to act as an antidote of Islamism in the ideological field. Nevertheless, the traditional ulama seem to represent a vanishing breed and the new generation of emerging scholars is more ambiguous in its attitude. In fact, after the decades of *da'wa*'s success, mainly supported by Haratines and other classes, *zwāya* seem the major advocates for a new wave of Islamists, chiefly political and involving Salafists and jihadists. At the same time, the *zwāya*, through their *maḥaḍra,* continue to feed moderate Islamism and the official religious personnel (administrative and political body). Islamism, on the other hand, seems to have brought significant support to the *zwāya* in strengthening and expanding their values among society. Islamism has also enabled Haratines' social advancement whereas *zwāya* have exploited it politically. Broadly, the Islamist revival has strengthened *zwāya* throughout the attraction exerted by religious values among Moorish society.

Overall, Nouakchott seems to have emerged from a relatively rigorous period, that of the last two decades. Today secular music is attracting more and more interest, particularly in taxis and in numerous media. On the other hand, the organization of social outings with religious entertainment on the periphery of the city has become a new social phenomenon. Haratines, having "found" religion and being educated in Islamic duties, are increasingly attracted by the material aspects of life with a predilection for the artistic heritage of Moorish society, such as poetry and music. Meanwhile, the *Banū Ḥassān* groups develop into target shooting parties (*šāra*), a characteristic activity of warriors in the past. One can ask if the revival of such ancient practices is a reaction to *maraboutisation*? If so, these trends raise the legitimate question of whether this whole social stream would stay aside with the religious aspects mentioned above in the public space of Nouakchott as a new form of social *modus vivendi.*

## Bibliography

An-Naʾim, A. Ahmed. *Islam and the State: Negotiating the Future of Shariʾa.* London: Harvard University Press, 2009.

Antil, Alain, "Contestation islamiste en Mauritanie: Menace ou bouc émissaire?" *Rapport Moyen-Orient/Afrique du Nord* 41 (2005): 35 pp.

Asad, Talal. *Formations of the Secular*. Stanford, Calif.: Stanford University Press, 2003.

———. *Genealogies of Religions: Discipline and Reasons of Power in Christianity and Islam*. Baltimore: Johns Hopkins University Press, 1993.

*Atlas de Nouakchott, Infrastructures et services urbains*. Saint-Étienne: Communauté Urbaine de Nouakchott, 2011.

Bourdieu, Pierre. "Social Space and Symbolic Power." *Sociological Theory* 7 (1989): 14–25.

———. "Sociologues de la croyance et croyance de sociologues." http://www.persee.fr/web/revues/home/prescript/issue/assr_0335–5985_1987_num_64_2: 155–61.

Brown, L. Carl. "Bourguiba and Bourguibism Revisited: Reflections and Interpretations." *Middle East Journal* 55 (2001): 43–57.

Casanova, José. *Public Religion in the Modern World.* Chicago: University of Chicago Press, 1994.

Charqi, Abdel Majid. *Al-Islām wa al-Ḥadāṯa, Dār al-Ğanūb li al-Našr*. Tunis, 2006.

Choplin, Armelle. "From the Chinguitti Mosque to Dubai Towers 'Extraversion,' Connections and Neo-Urban Society in a Globalized Mauritania." *Maghreb Review* 35 (2010): 146–63.

———. *Nouakchott au carrefour de la Mauritanie et du monde.* Clamecy: Karthalla-Prodig, 2009.

Geertz, Clifford. *The Interpretation of Cultures*. New York: Basic Books, 1973.

Glew, Robert S. "A Discourse-Centred Approach Toward Understanding Muslim Identities in Zinder." *Islam et Sociétés au Sud du Sahara* 14–15 (2000–2001): 99–119.

Hirschkind, Charles. www.columbia.edu/cu/cup/catalog/data/023113/0231138180.htm. New York: Columbia University Press, 2006.

Islamic Republic of Mauritania, Ministry of Islamic Affairs and Original Teaching. *Report Summary of General Survey of maḥaḍra and Mosque 2009/2010.* Nouakchott, July 2010.

Jourde, Cedric. "Ethnicity, Democratization, and Political Dramas: Insights into Ethnic Politics in Mauritania." *African Issues* 29 (2001): 26–30.

———. "Overlapping Solidarities: The Politics of Ethnicity and Sufi Turuq in Mauritania." *Maghreb Review* 35 (2010): 222–42.

———. "Sifting Through the Layers of Insecurity in the Sahel: The Case of Mauritania."*Africa Security Brief* 15 (2011): 1–7.

Kepel, G. *Muslim Extremism in Egypt: The Prophet and the Pharaoh.* Translated by John Rotschild. Berkeley: University of California Press, 1986.

Kerrou, Mohamed. *Hijâb: Nouveaux voiles et espaces publics.* Tunis: CERES, 2010.

Launay, Robert. *Beyond the Stream: Islam and Society in a West African Town.* Los Angeles: University of California Press, 1992.

Lesourd, C. "Le *Mesrah:* Regard sur la 'culture matérielle du succès' à Nouakchott." *L'Année du Maghreb* (online) 4 (October 2008).

Lukens-Bull, R. A. "Between Text and Practice: Considerations in the Anthropological Study of Islam." *Marburg Journal of Religion* 4 (1999): 1–21.

Munson, Henry, Jr. "The Social Base of Islamic Militancy in Morocco." *Middle East Journal* 40 (1986): 267–84.

Norris, H. T. *Saharian Myth and Saga.* London: Oxford University Press, 1972.

———. *Shinqiti Folk Literature and Song.* Oxford: Oxford University Press, 1968.

Nouhi, M. Lahbib. "Religion and Society in Saharan Tribes: Authority and Power in the Zawaya's Religious Culture." Ph.D. dissertation, University of Alberta, 2009.

Ould Abdel Latif, Mohamed Fall. *Al-Wālī al-Musāid lī sā.* Nouakchott: Dār al-Fikr, 2011.

Ould Ahmed Salem, Zekeria. "Archéologie d'un espace public délocalisé: Les Maures et St. Louis à travers les âges." In *Les trajectoires d'un état-frontière: Espaces, évolutions politiques et transformations sociales en Mauritanie,* edited by Zekeria Ould Ahmed Salem, 141–78 (Dakar: CODESRIA, 2004).

———. "Islam in Mauritania between Political Expansion and Globalization: Elites, Institutions, Knowledge, and Networks." In *Islam and Muslim Politics in Africa,* edited by Benjamin Soares and René Otayek, 27–46. New York: Palgrave Macmillan, 2007.

———. “Prêcher dans le désert: L’univers du Cheikh Sidi Yahya et l’évolution de l’Islamisme Mauritanien.” *Islam et Sociétés au Sud du Sahara* 14–15 (2000–2001): 5–40.

Ould Bara, Yahya. *Al-Mağmūʾa al-Kubrā al-šāmila li-fatāwā wa nawāzi lwa aḥkām ahl Ġarbwa Ğanūb al-Saḥrā :mudawwana min 6800 fatwā wa nāzila wa ḥukm.* Nouakchott: Al-Manār, 2009.

———. “Fiqh, société et pouvoir: Préoccupations et soucis des théologiens maures du XVIIème au XXème siècle.” Ph.D. dissertation, Ecole des Hautes Etudes en Sciences Sociales, 2000.

———. “*L’Islam en ville: Réseaux de solidarité, réseaux politiques*.” Paper presented at IRD Workshop, “*La ville ou l’état*,” Rouen, 2003.

———. “Mutations des formes de religiosité: Sources et débats.” In *Les trajectoires d’un état-frontière: Espaces, évolutions politiques et transformations sociales en Mauritanie*, edited by Zekeria Ould Ahmed Salem, 207–39. Dakar: CODESRIA, 2004.

Ould Cheikh, Abdel Wedoud. “Mutations de l’espace public et nouvelles formes de citoyenneté: La difficile sortie des débats sur l’esclavage en Mauritanie.” In *Les trajectoires d’un état-frontière: Espaces, évolutions politiques et transformations sociales en Mauritanie*, edited by Zekeria Ould Ahmed Salem, 281–304. Dakar: CODESRIA, 2004.

———. “Nomadisme, Islam et pouvoir politique dans la société maure précoloniale (XIè–XIXè).” Ph.D. dissertation, Paris V, 1985.

OuldEthmane Sid Ahmed Yessa, Abdel Nasser. “L’opposition politique en Mauritanie: Discours et mode d’action depuis 1980.” Mémoire de maîtrise, Université de Nouakchott, 1987.

Ould Mahfoudh, Habib. “Mauritanides.”*Mauritanie Demain* 19 (1991): 4.

———. “Mauritanides.” *Le Calame* 242 (1998): 4–5.

Park, Mungo. *The Journal of a Mission to the Interior of Africa: In Year 1805*. London: printed for John Murray, 1815.

Pitte, J.-R. *Nouakchott, capitale de la Mauritanie*. Paris: Sorbonne, 1977.

Schulz, E. Dorothea. “Promises of (Im)mediate Salvation: Islam, Broadcast Media, and the Remaking of Religious Experience in Mali.” *American Ethnologist* 33 (2006): 210–29.

Simard, Gisèle. *Petites commerçantes de Mauritanie, voiles, perles et henné.* Paris: Karthala, 2000.

Stewart, C. C. *Islam and Social Order in Mauritania: A Case Study from the Nineteenth Century*. Oxford: Clarendon, 1973.

Waltz, Susan. “Islamist Appeal in Tunisia.”*Middle East Journal* 40 (1986): 651–70.

Wane, Saidou. "Usages du téléphone moblile et changements sociaux chez les Imraguin du banc d'Arguin, cas de Mamghar (Mauritanie)." Master's dissertation, Université Paris Descartes, Paris, 2009.

Wuld Mazid, Mohamed al-Amīn. *Al-Ḥaraka al-Islāmiya fī Muritānya*, link at www.ak-akhbar.info, archives November, 28, 2010.

Zubaida, Sami. *Beyond Islam*. New York: IB Tauris, 2011.

# *SOURCES*

# Developing Materials for a Digital Library Gallery

*Catherine Foley*, MICHIGAN STATE UNIVERSITY

DOI: 10.5192/21540993050183

**Abstract**

*This essay explores how scholars working on "Pluralism and Adaptation in the Islamic Practice of Senegal and Ghana," a National Endowment for the Humanities (NEH) Collaborative Research project, partnered with a digital humanities center to create freely available online digital collections to enhance research, teaching, and learning about West African Islam. By looking closely at the development of one of these online galleries, Professor David Robinson's "Failed Islamic States in the Senegambia," we examine how materials are prepared for this type of web presentation. Specifically, the essay reviews the efforts of subject experts in describing and cataloging multimedia collections so that users understand the context in which the primary source materials were created, as well as the overarching purpose of the digital collections. We also describe the technology and standards used for storing, retrieving, and displaying interviews, documents, and images in this collection. In short, this essay provides insight into the processes and challenges by which we transform field and archival research data into contextualized web resources useful for learning about and researching Africa and Islam.*

*Islamic Africa*, VOL. 5, NO. 1, 2014. ISSN 2154-0993.  www.islamicafricajournal.org

## *Background*

As is evident from the annotated webography compiled by Peter Limb for this issue of *Islamic Africa*, the number of digital libraries focused on Islam in Africa has been increasing in recent years. As part of this trend, Africanist scholars at Michigan State University (MSU) and Indiana University have partnered with Matrix: The Center for Digital Humanities and Social Sciences at MSU and collaborators from Harvard, James Madison, and Boston universities to create free multimedia digital libraries of research materials collected by scholars in the field. Funding for these digital libraries was provided by TICFIA, the Technological Innovation and Cooperation for Foreign Information Access program of the Department of Education, for "Diversity and Tolerance in the Islam of West Africa: Creating Online Resources of Peaceful Muslim Practice in Senegal and Ghana" (2005–9) and the NEH Collaborative Research grant program for "Pluralism and Adaptation in the Islamic Practice of Senegal and Ghana" (2009–13) and "Islam and Modernity: Alternatives in Contemporary Senegambia and Ghana" (2012–15). The latest efforts, many of which are described in David Robinson's article in this issue, include online galleries of photos, maps, archival documents, and interviews in audio or video formats (some with transcripts or translations) focused on Muslim communities in Senegal and Ghana. Collaborating scholars contextualized these collections with explanatory introductions and interpretive frames as well as with detailed item-level descriptions of primary sources. In the process, our partners, who are engaged scholars, have also become co-curators with Matrix of online rich media galleries intended for teaching, learning, and even research. Generously, they have published their research data in digital libraries, making it available free of charge to academic and non-academic users around the world for further investigation, analysis, and interpretation.

David Robinson's "Failed Islamic States" gallery sheds light on the materials development process. This online collection about eighteenth- and nineteenth-century reformers who "sought to extend the breadth and depth of Islamic practice in Senegambia and neighboring areas by using the 'jihad of the sword'" is a valuable touchstone for this essay for three reasons. First, Robinson elaborates on his analysis in this issue (see "Muslim Societies in West Africa: Historical and Contemporary Perspectives in Digital Form"), which explains the significance and value of the materials in his gallery. Second, Robinson's collection represents the most complete gallery in "Pluralism and Adaptation in the Islamic Practice of Senegal and Ghana," an NEH project still under active development. In other words, it is the most current example of our digital library production around African content. Third, "Failed Islamic States" features a rich variety of material types: 12 documents, 13 images, 3 excerpted interviews with Pulaar transcripts and English translations, 4 maps, and a backbone narrative made up of 5 essays that analyze the sources and contextualize the collection. Together the resources in "Failed Islamic States" provide opportunities for reflecting on the exciting and challenging processes of transforming research data into meaningful digital libraries aimed at promoting research, learning, and teaching about Islam and Africa.

Before delving into the materials development process for "Failed Islamic States,"[1] it is worthwhile to click through the online gallery to become familiar with the collection and website features. A brief tour of the gallery should provide a general frame of reference for the forthcoming description of the materials preparation process.

## *Materials Preparation*

There are a number of steps we take to bring scholarship and research materials into an open-access digital library. Materials preparation is a convenient shorthand I use for the main steps of deploying standards-based tools and technology to transform content for end-user access. In the materials preparation process, scholars and Matrix collaborate to (1) describe individual primary sources; (2) analyze and synthesize research materials, thereby providing interpretive frames for non-expert audiences to understand the collection; (3) store newly collected and created resources in a digital repository or database; and (4) share or publish digital collections on the web. These steps, which broadly encompass describing, storing, and sharing research data, are most effectively carried out by using best practices in digital libraries, including the creation of meaningful metadata.

### Metadata

Metadata describes other data like primary sources and research data in structured or standardized ways in order to make it easier to store, locate,

[1] "Failed Islamic States in the Senegambia," http://www.aodl.org/islamicpluralism/failedislamicstates/.

access, use, and reuse these resources. Metadata is like a label on a tin can in the grocery store that explains if the can contains soup or sardines, describes the ingredients, and communicates nutrition facts and sell-by dates. Most people would not buy a can without a label because they would not know what the product was or even if it was safe to use. Like the label on a tin can, metadata in the digital library context conveys important information about the materials stored in the library, including the title and a description of the resource, who created the item, and when. Other metadata records details about the file format of the digital resource: for example, if an interview is an audio file in MP3 or a video interview in MP4, as well as any copyright or permission statements that explain the terms of use for the digital item.

How metadata is structured is very important because it establishes a common understanding about the meaning of the data and ensures the correct and proper use of the information by creators and users. For digital libraries at Matrix, we use the Dublin Core Metadata Element Set (Dublin Core) to describe the research data and primary sources.[2] Dublin Core is an International Organization for Standardization "cross-domain resource description" standard. It includes 15 metadata elements or fields that capture a variety of information about digital resources. At Matrix, we consistently use 12 of the 15 core elements, specifically Title, Creator, Description, Publisher, Contributor, Date, Type, Format, Source, Language, Rights, and Identifier. As necessary, on a project-by-project basis, we may also include the other three Dublin Core elements in the database, Relation, Subject, and Coverage.

Each metadata element is defined and maintained on the Dublin Core website with suggestions for using additional specifications to further structure the data. For example, some digital libraries use subject terms and name authorities developed by the Library of Congress to uniformly identify the intellectual content or topic of a resource or to ensure the uniform spelling for names of people associated with a resource.

## Describing Primary Sources

David Robinson and other scholars who collaborated on the "Pluralism and Adaptation in the Islamic Practice of Senegal and Ghana" project created a database record made up of Dublin Core metadata for each document,

[2] "Dublin Core Metadata Element Set," dublincore.org/documents/dces/.

image, interview, and map in their respective online galleries. This aspect of materials preparation is a step more involved than the usual work researchers invest in documenting and referencing supporting evidence. Because the audience of "Failed Islamic States" includes scholars and non-specialists alike, the metadata must be written so that it can be understood not only within and connected to the "Failed Islamic States" gallery but also independent of it. Therefore, the Dublin Core Description of a document must be general enough so that a non-specialist can keyword search for it. Further descriptions and all other metadata must be free from interpretation. That way, if someone stumbles across the document in a Google search, the user will be able to understand what the resource is in its own right without consulting Robinson's analysis for context. This type of metadata creation encourages repurposing of the materials for other galleries or exhibits that have nothing to do with Robinson's original motivation behind the research and the resulting digital library. It can also lead to the reuse of the primary sources by students or other scholars for completely different research questions and analyses.

## Analyzing Primary Sources to Create an Interpretive Frame

At the heart of Robinson's "Failed Islamic States" gallery is a backbone narrative that examines the unsuccessful efforts of Muslim reformers like Umar Tall (ca. 1797–1864) and his son, Ahmed al-Kabir (ca. 1864–1893), and the Madiyankoobe of northwestern Senegal (1860s–1870s), to establish Islamic states through military force. Robinson's analysis has in-text references to the supporting primary source materials and embedded links to the sources themselves, which are described and stored as records in the digital repository for the project.

The five essays that make up the backbone narrative serve as a frame for understanding the maps, images, documents, and interviews in this digital library. Through the essays, Robinson articulates the parameters of the collection and explains how and why these resources are related and why users should care about these relationships. In short, the essays provide an interpretive frame for understanding the collection. Further, the presentation of an essay married to the research data invites users to immediately interact with the supporting research rather than chasing down footnotes and references for later investigation. Instantaneously, users can consult the primary sources to see how Robinson supports his interpretation and analysis. We deliberately used this presentation model in order to offer users opportunities for engaging in discussions about scholarly analysis and to encourage the interrogation of primary sources.

## Storing Resources in a Digital Repository

We use KORA to manage and curate all digital libraries at Matrix, including "Failed Islamic States." KORA is a digital collection management system used to create and maintain digital repositories and libraries, store multimedia collections, and curate online exhibits. After Robinson described items in his collection with Dublin Core metadata, we moved these materials (digital files and metadata) into KORA to secure them and make them available on the web. For more than a decade, Matrix has been developing and maintaining KORA with grant funding from the National Science Foundation, NEH, and the U.S. Department of Education.

KORA is an open-source application. Matrix has published KORA's source code under a GNU General Public License, version 2. In short, KORA is free software, which allows it to be used, modified, and shared. It is built on a system of free and open-source software including an Apache web server and a MySQL database, with PHP applications for dynamic web page delivery.[3] Through a browser-based dashboard, like WordPress, users, including the scholars collaborating on our NEH project, can work in the database to create, store, and manage their multimedia files and associated metadata. Matrix hosts digital files and metadata stored in KORA on Matrix servers, which we routinely back up as part of Matrix's disaster mitigation plan.

## Sharing Digital Collections on the Web

From the project's inception, creating digital resources for teaching, learning, and researching Islamic practices in West Africa has driven the layout of gallery pages and shaped our thinking about how best to connect and publish related materials on the website. To give users ample opportunity to interact with and examine the primary sources in the collections, we have embedded images and documents in the backbone analytical essays and listed all supporting materials, including interviews, in the left column of the essay pages. See, for example, Robinson's essay on Umar

[3] "LAMP (software bundle)," http://en.wikipedia.org/wiki/LAMP_%28software_bundle%29.

Tall,[4] which has 2 interviews, 2 images, 7 documents, and 2 maps. Displaying the content in this way on one page, a student or researcher can immediately confront Robinson's evidence and not just the excerpts he used to support his analysis and conclusions. This presentation model offers students, teachers, and other researchers opportunities to evaluate the merits of the scholarship and to discuss the use of sources.

Transferring Robinson's intellectual labor on the essays to the website required two additional steps. First, we used a tool in the KORA repository to connect or *associate* the analytical essay to the primary source materials and metadata in the database. This KORA "associator tool" created concrete links between the essays and the supporting interviews and maps in the database and defined the relationship between these materials as analysis linked to the evidence. As a result of these associations in the database, a new resource, a composite of linked materials, is created and available for display on the site.

Second, through custom programming and design, we deliver and format "Failed Islamic States" content on the website. A cadre of undergraduate computer science students at Matrix writes PHP code that connects to KORA to retrieve the appropriate digital files and metadata for a specific page. Using HTML and JavaScript, a designer, often in collaboration with a programmer, structures the KORA content into columns, tables, or lists (as required for a page) and then, with Cascading Style Sheets (CSS), describes the visual presentation specifying the fonts, colors, and layout. In this way, we pull the analytical essays from KORA and display them in a purposeful way on the website, creating a captivating media experience intended to enhance the users' understanding of the collection and to facilitate user interaction with the materials in the gallery. In sum, after an essay is crafted, the analysis and evidence must be combined in KORA before it can be retrieved from the database and presented on the website in a meaningful manner.

## *Conclusion*

Collaboration is a key to transforming research data into contextualized web resources for learning about and researching Africa and Islam. Developing materials for these online collections depends on the intellectual

[4] "Umar Tall or al-hajj Umar," http://aodl.org/islamicpluralism/failedislamicstates/essays/43-1A9-F/.

insights of subject experts like David Robinson as well as digital library best practices such as standards-based resource descriptions (e.g., Dublin Core). By describing individual items with meaningful metadata and analyzing these resources in the backbone narrative, scholars provide interpretive frames to contextualize the collections for non-specialist audiences, like students. Matrix brings technological expertise to the academic partnership, leveraging established technologies like the KORA digital repository, PHP, JavaScript, HTML, and CSS to store and share the resources. Together subject and technology specialists co-create sustainable, rich media exhibits that promote teaching, learning, and research inside *and* outside the academy.

The benefits of these digital library collaborations outnumber the challenges encountered so far. The technological infrastructure is well supported. Notably, there is MSU-wide institutional commitment to providing continued access to the content stored in the KORA digital repository. Instead, the challenge is to maintain the vitality of sites, to update them in the face of rapid technological change on the web. This requires funding that is not readily available.

Despite the challenges, Matrix continues to pursue opportunities to develop freely available digital libraries as part of its broader mission to promote the democratization of knowledge and the production of new scholarship. Thematically coherent collections invite users to learn more about Africa, to ask and answer new research questions, and to reinterpret the collections. The willingness of our partners to share their field and archival research contributes to collaborative research models in which scholars share their data rather than squirreling it away. As a result, our digital library efforts support learning about Islam, Africa, and the world and simultaneously contribute to the production of new scholarship through resource sharing.

# Islamic Africa: A Select, Annotated Webography

*Peter Limb*, MICHIGAN STATE UNIVERSITY

DOI: 10.5192/21540993050191

**Abstract**

*In this brief essay and webography, I indicate ways to pursue the themes of Islamic Africa on the Web. Digital and online libraries about Islam and West Africa, and more broadly about the history and culture of predominantly Islamic parts of Africa, have been steadily growing in the last few years. To assist readers of* Islamic Africa *to appreciate the span of these rapidly expanding resources and their depth and usefulness, and hopefully to make use of them in learning or researching Islam in Africa, I present this select survey of digital resources.*

## *Selection Criteria, Scope, and Arrangement*

In selecting resources, so as to facilitate the widest access to scholarly resources, I have given priority to "open source" sites that anyone may access. However, the exigencies of contemporary publishing and maintaining large amounts of data mean that a range of both proprietary and member-only resources now exist on Islam in Africa, and these are included. They are marked with an asterisk or double asterisk respectively. The emphasis is on scholarly resources. I have drawn

*Islamic Africa,* VOL. 5, NO. 1, 2014. ISSN 2154-0993.  www.islamicafricajournal.org

in particular on web resources on Africa indexed in guides at three universities.[1]

The geographical and chronological scope of this select survey of digital resources is primarily West (or western) Africa, and the nineteenth and twentieth centuries. A few select resources on wider Islamic sources across Africa also are included.

The arrangement divides into three sections: (1) West Africa, (2) Other parts of Africa, (3) General resources.

Some qualifications are necessary. The resources described below are generally available online, either by open access or by subscription/ purchase or membership of an institution such as the Center for Research Libraries (based in the United States, with a handful of African members). However, for many repositories in Africa it is expensive to connect to the Internet or allow easy access from the North to scanned archives and other material. As a result, there are some sources (for example, theses and archives at UCAD in Dakar, National Archives of Zambia, and University of Malawi) that exist in a digital form, and may be used in-house, but are not "online" in terms of the Internet or even in some cases beyond the institution. Some such materials may be made available to partners in the North or in various formats elsewhere. There is some overlap in the entries below. In addition, some collections are projects which are in progress and not yet available.

The communities and audiences served by the sites vary. Those proprietary and member-only resources detailed below are available chiefly to scholarly communities such as universities. Open-access sites obviously have the widest potential users in mind, such that the interested general public, as well as specialists of Islam, are served, as are indeed members of both groups on the African continent.

The types of resources discussed also vary considerably in nature and

---

[1] Columbia University, Michigan State University, and Stanford University. See Yuusuf Caruso, "Religion in Africa on the Internet" in African Studies Internet Resources (http://library.columbia.edu/locations/global/virtual-libraries/african_studies/religion.html); Peter Limb with Ibra Sene, Islam pages of "An A-Z of African Studies on the Internet" (Michigan State: http://staff.lib.msu.edu/limb/a-z/az_hm2.html); Karen Fung, "Islam in Africa" section of "Africa South of the Sahara" (Stanford: http://www-sul.stanford.edu/depts/ssrg/africa/religion/islam-in-africa.html). For more popular websites, for instance on the Tijani Sufi Brotherhood, see the list maintained by Yuusuf Caruso.

potential. Some are very much selections from much wider sources and as such offer only a tantalizing taste of the universe of available primary source material. This limitation is to be expected in the "pilot study" nature of many grant-based projects from which some of these sites have emerged. However, these trailblazing products have laid down a foundation upon which interested communities can build more substantial and comprehensive publications to better serve serious scholars. To do so effectively requires the consistent deployment over time of substantial human and capital resources, and suggests the need for the cooperation of publishers, libraries, and academics. Indeed, the vulnerability of many archives of the African Islamic world to extremes of climate, administrative neglect induced by limited financial resources, and political conflict make this urgent.

We can glimpse the possibilities attainable by such cooperation in sites detailed below that serve up an entire archive such as, for example, the World Newspaper Archive, which presents entire historic runs of African newspapers. However, for West and East Africa this is currently limited to newspapers in European languages, which in any case are few and far between before the early part of the twentieth century. The steady and more comprehensive digitization of more sources in Arabic, *ajami,* and African languages would open up fruitful terrain for researchers.

Available formats for viewing or listening to such sources include textual (such as PDF), visual, and audio resources. The ability to search and manipulate PDFs in a scholarly fashion is a great boon to researchers, and enables, for instance, investigation of particular themes and terms across different languages. When this is combined with effective search engines, for example, presenting search results in thumbnail format so the researcher can immediately see the context of a term, the scholarly process is expedited. To do this effectively, enhanced searching of PDFs in Arabic and *ajami* scripts is a priority. The spoken sphere is extremely important in African oral cultures that have long transmitted the Islamic heritage. The great potential of online audiovisual technology to preserve and efficiently deliver to scholars such orality is well captured in the coordinated scrolling text and audio sources in Fula and French languages presented in the "Saint-Louis: Religious Pluralism in the Heart of Senegal" pages of the African Online Digital Library, the first-mentioned site detailed below.

## *Webography*

(* = proprietary; ** = member-only)

### West Africa

African Online Digital Library[2] (Michigan State University)

A range of projects on Islam, described separately below: Collection Boubacar Barry; "Passport to Paradise": Sufi Arts of Senegal and Beyond; Mosques of Bondoukou; Fuuta Tooro Oral History Project; Ajami in the Senegambia; L'Institut Fondemental d'Afrique Noire; Diversity and Tolerance in the Islam of West Africa;[3] Pluralism and Adaptation in the Islamic Practice of Senegal and Ghana.[4] We have drawn on these extensively in David Robinson's and Catherine Foley's essays in this issue. The African Online Digital Library is housed and maintained at Matrix, the Center for Digital Humanities and Social Sciences at Michigan State University.

Arabic Manuscripts from West Africa: A Catalog of the Herskovits Library Collection[5]

Online catalog of an important collection of Arabic script materials from West Africa (over 5,000 items) from the Melville J. Herskovits Library of African Studies, Northwestern University, comprising the Umar Falke, John Paden, John Hunwick, and University of Ghana Collections.

Recueil de textes concernant l'histoire du Soudan[6]**

Compilation from Fonds Archinard in the Bibliothèque Nationale, Département des Manuscrits: On populations of the Sahara; significant fragments concerning the history of Tombouctou; fragments of Fatassi by Mahmadou Koti, and so on (online for members of the Center for Research Libraries).

West African Arabic Manuscript Project[7]

Arabic Manuscript Management System, English-Arabic bibliographic tool of 23,000+ West African Arabic manuscript citations from collections

---

[2] "African Online Digital Library," http://www.aodl.org.

[3] "Diversity and Tolerance in the Islam of West Africa," http://aodl.org/islamictolerance.

[4] "Pluralism and Adaptation in the Islamic Practice of Senegal and Ghana," http://aodl.org/islamicpluralism.

[5] A Catalog of the Herskovits Library Collection," http://digital.library.northwestern.edu/arbmss/index.html.

[6] "Recueil de textes concernant l'histoire du Soudan," http://dds.crl.edu/CRLdelivery.asp?tid=16993.

[7] "West African Arabic Manuscript Project," http://www.westafricanmanuscripts.org.

across the Sahel. Edited by C. C. Stewart and Bruce Stewart Hall. "Experimental linkage of digital images of manuscript texts . . . is currently underway."

GAMBIA

Safeguarding Gambia, Casamance, and Guinea-Bissau's Oral Histories: The Oral History Archive at Fajara, The Gambia[8]

National Centre for Arts and Culture, Banjul: will digitize "recordings and their transcriptions of interviews with elders" from Gambia, Casamance, Guinea-Bissau. Some content on Islam including Soninke-Marabout wars.[9] (Endangered Archives Project 536: in progress.)

Social History of the Gambia: Rescuing an Endangered Archive, Police and Court Records[10]

National Records Services, The Gambia. Includes: Court of Requests, Mohammedan Court, Police/Magistrates Courts, Supreme Court Collections.[11] (Endangered Archives Project 231: completed, not yet online, but available within British Library.)

GHANA

Everyday Islam in Kumasi: Devout Lay Men and Women in Daily Life,[12] by Gracia Clark.

Maps, images, audio/video interviews, essays, texts related to Muslim men and women who live and work in Kumasi, Ghana. Part of African Online Digital Library.

[8] "Safeguarding Gambia, Casamance and Guinea-Bissau's Oral Histories: The Oral History Archive at Fajara, The Gambia," http://eap.bl.uk/database/overview_project.a4d?projID=EAP536;r=15724.

[9] Toby Green, King's College London and the National Centre for Arts and Culture, The Gambia.

[10] Walter Hawthorne, Michigan State University and National Records Services, the Gambia. "Social History of the Gambia: Rescuing an Endangered Archive, Police and Court Records," http://eap.bl.uk/database/overview_project.a4d?projID=EAP231;r=24484.

[11] "MATRIX and Department of History," Michigan State University. Thanks to Bala Saho and Assan Saar for their comments. For a video (4 mins. 32 secs.) on the project see http://www2.matrix.msu.edu/2010/08/matrix-and-msu-department-of-history-partner-in-the-gambia.

[12] "Everyday Islam in Kumasi: Devout Lay Men and Women in Daily Life," http://aodl.org/islamictolerance/kumasi.

H-West-Africa[13] (H-Net)
Electronic discussion list open to all interested in West African history and culture.

## Mali

Ancient Manuscripts from the Desert Libraries of Timbuktu[14] (Library of Congress)
Sixteenth to eighteenth-century manuscripts from Mamma Haidara Commemorative Library and Library of Cheick Zayni Baye of Boujbeha.

Islamic Manuscripts from Mali[15] (Library of Congress)
32 manuscripts from Mamma Haidara Commemorative Library and Library of Cheick Zayni Baye of Boujbeha, Timbuktu "presented online are displayed in their entirety."

Project to Digitize and Preserve the Manuscripts of Djenné and Surrounding Villages[16]
Aims to digitize 150,000+ pages of manuscripts (chiefly 1700–1900) at Djenné Manuscript Library.[17] (Endangered Archives Project 690: in progress.)

Slavery and Manumission Manuscripts of Timbuktu[18]
Full text. "From the Bibliothèque Commémorative Mama Haidara in Timbuktu, Mali, a collection of 19th-century manuscripts relating to slavery and manumission in Timbuktu. The materials, in Arabic, provide documentation on Africans in slavery in Muslim societies."

## Nigeria

Early Nigerian Qurʾānic Manuscripts (ENiQMa):[19] An Interdisciplinary Study of the Kanuri Glosses and Arabic Commentaries
Project in progress (SOAS).

---

13 "H-West Africa (H-Net)," https://networks.h-net.org/h-west-africa.

14 "Ancient Manuscripts from the Desert Libraries of Timbuktu," http://www.loc.gov/exhibits/mali/mali-exhibit.html.

15 "Islamic Manuscripts from Mali," http://international.loc.gov/intldl/malihtml.

16 "Project to Digitise and Preserve the Manuscripts of Djenné and Surrounding Villages," http://eap.bl.uk/database/overview_project.a4d?projID=EAP690;r=41.

17 Sophie Sarin and La Bibliothèque de Manuscrits de Djenné, http://www.djennemanuscrits.com.

18 "Slavery and Manumission Manuscripts of Timbuktu," http://ecollections.crl.edu/cdm4/index_timbuktu.php?CISOROOT=/timbuktu.

19 "Early Nigerian Qurʾānic Manuscripts (ENiQMa): An Interdisciplinary Study of the Kanuri Glosses and Arabic Commentaries," http://www.soas.ac.uk/africa/research/kanuri.

Northern Nigeria: Precolonial Documents Preservation Scheme[20]

Online files of select Arabic manuscripts held by Kano State History and Culture Bureau "relating to the precolonial history of the Kano emirate," chiefly "letters written by prominent judges, Emirs and leaders."[21] (Endangered Archives Project 087.)

Old Kanembu Islamic Manuscripts Collection[22] (SOAS Digital Library)

"One of the earliest written sub-Saharan languages . . . The collection represents Old Kanembu marginal and interlinear annotations in both Qurʾanic and non-Qurʾanic manuscripts."

Safeguarding Fulfulde *Ajami* Manuscripts of Nigerian Jihad Poetry by Usman dan Fodio (1754–1817) and Contemporaries[23]

Will digitize 93 manuscripts of Fulfulde jihad poetry of ʾYola, Nigeria (poems by Usman dan Fodio and his daughter Nana Asmaʾu).[24] (Endangered Archives Project 387: in progress.)

## Senegal

*Ajami* in the Senegambia[25]

By Fallou Ngom. Over 20 *ajami* manuscripts and video[26] produced by West African scholars. Part of the African Online Digital Library. See also Wolofal Manuscripts, Senegal.[27]

---

[20] "Northern Nigeria: Precolonial Documents Preservation Scheme," http://eap.bl.uk/database/results.a4d?projID=EAP087;r=18467.

[21] Mohammed Salau, York University, Canada, and Arewa House, Kaduna. For example, it includes "Digital images of the text of a lesson given by the Prophet Muhammad (S.A.W.) addressing the people of the world, calling them to the Islamic religion. Date of copy unknown," http://eap.bl.uk/database/overview_item.a4d?catId=20273;r=16827.

[22] "Old Kanembu Islamic Manuscripts Collection," http://www.soas.ac.uk/africa/research/oldkanembu.

[23] "Safeguarding Fulfulde Ajami Manuscripts of Nigerian Jihad poetry by Usman dan Fodio (1754–1817) and Contemporaries," http://eap.bl.uk/database/overview_project.a4d?projID=EAP387;r=26869.

[24] Anneke Breedveld, Tilburg University, and owner of the poetry.

[25] "Ajami in the Senegambia," http://aodl.org/islamictolerance/ajami.

[26] "Serigne Mouhamadou Masokhna Loʾs Wolof Ajami Multimedia Presentation," in "Ajami in the Senegambia," http://aodl.org/islamictolerance/ajami/presentation.php?kid=3B-182-5.

[27] "Wolofal Manuscripts, Senegal," Boston University Libraries Open BU, http://open.bu.edu/xmlui/handle/2144/2381.

Collection Boubacar Barry[28]

Historical writings on the Futa Jalon. From the African Online Digital Library. Part of the African Online Digital Library.

Failed Islamic States in Senegambia[29]

By David Robinson, featuring leaders of reform movements in the nineteenth century, after the founding of the Almamate of Futa Toro, with a concentration on al-hajj Umar and his son Ahmad al-Kabir.

Fuuta Tooro Oral History Project[30]

Interviews with the Tokolor or Fulbe informants; original sound (Pulaar) and English and French translations; collected by David Robinson in 1968–69; only 3 of his interviews are available here. Part of the African Online Digital Library.

Medina Baay Research Association[31]

Compiled by Joseph Hill. Includes texts, interviews, and photographs on the Ibrahimiyyah branch of the Tijaniyya Sufi order founded by Baay Ñas.

Passport to Paradise: Visualizing Islam in West Africa and the Mouride Diaspora[32] (UCLA Fowler Museum of Cultural History)

Online exhibition on "arts of the Mourides, a mystical Muslim movement originating in Senegal, West Africa." A selection is also at the African Online Digital Library.[33]

Projet Majalis[34] (Dakar, Sénégal)

Murid Sufi Brotherhood (La Mouridiyya) followers of Cheikh Ahmadou Bamba. Includes articles and videos. Interface in English,[35] French, and Wolof.[36]

Saint-Louis: Religious Pluralism in the Heart of Senegal[37]

"Handwritten texts, images and audio interviews dealing with the interactions of Saint Louis's French Catholic communities, the Muslim majority,

---

[28] "Collection Boubacar Barry," http://aodl.org/westafrica/barry.php.

[29] "Failed Islamic States in Senegambia," part of "Pluralism and Adaptation in the Islamic Practices of Senegal and Ghana," http://aodl.org/islamicpluralism/failedislamicstates.

[30] "Fuuta Tooro Oral History Project," http://aodl.org/westafrica/futa2.php.

[31] "Medina Baay Research Association," http://medinabaay.org.

[32] "Passport to Paradise: Visualizing Islam in West Africa and the Mouride Diaspora," http://www.fowler.ucla.edu/passporttoparadise.htm.

[33] "Passport to Paradise," http://aodl.org/westafrica/passport.php.

[34] "Projet Majalis," http://www.majalis.org/index3.php?nav=n.

[35] "Projet Majalis," http://www.majalis.org/indexlg1.php?langue=en.

[36] "Projet Majalis," http://www.majalis.org/indexlg1.php?langue=wf.

[37] "Saint-Louis: Religious Pluralism in the Heart of Senegal," http://aodl.org/islamictolerance/saintlouis.

the French administration, and Freemasons in the late 19th and 20th centuries." Part of the African Online Digital Library.

Wolofal Manuscripts, Senegal[38]

29 manuscripts from 15 collections in Wolofal (Wolof Ajami) by Muridiyya sufis. Includes "satirical, polemical, and protest poetry, as well as biographies, eulogies, genealogies, talismanic resources, therapeutic medical manuals, historical records, instructions on codes of conduct, translation (with commentaries) of the Qur'an and volumes of the internal biography of Ahmadou Bamba." Copies at West African Research Center (Dakar), British Library, and Boston University digital repository.[39] Parts incorporated in *Ajami* in the Senegambia in the African Online Digital Library.

West African Online Digital Library[40]

Galleries of photographs, audio interviews, and documents contributed by scholars, with research about best practices for international, multilingual digital repositories. Includes: Sampling from L'Institut Fondemental d'Afrique Noire.[41] "A sample of the work currently being undertaken at IFAN to digitize their vast collection." Part of the African Online Digital Library.

West African Research Association[42] (WARA)

Includes Rethinking Islam in West Africa: Legal, Political and Artistic Perspectives (lecture series; some in streaming video) and the WARC Library of Congress Bibliography.

## Other Regions of Africa (Selected)

### Cameroon

Bamum Script and Archives Project: Saving Africa's Written Heritage[43]

Over 7,000 documents transcribed in Bamum script. Includes some commentaries on Islam. Content not yet online (Endangered Archives Project 051).[44]

---

[38] "Wolofal Manuscripts, Senegal," http://open.bu.edu/xmlui/handle/2144/2381.

[39] Fallou Ngom, Boston University, and West African Research Center, Dakar.

[40] "West African Digital Library," http://aodl.org/westafrica.

[41] "Sampling from L'Institut Fondemental d'Afrique Noire," http://aodl.org/westafrica/ifan.php.

[42] "West African Research Association," http://www.bu.edu/wara.

[43] "Bamum Script and Archives Project: Saving Africa's Written Heritage," http://eap.bl.uk/database/overview_project.a4d?projID=EAP051;r=23811.

[44] Konrad Tuchscherer, St. John's University, New York, and Archives du Palais des Rois Bamoun.

### Kenya

The Manuscripts of the Riyadh Mosque of Lamu, Kenya[45]
130 manuscripts (1837–1920) of "one of the oldest continuously functioning Islamic teaching institutions in East Africa." Digital copies at Riyadha Mosque; Kenya Museum, Lamu; Kenya National Museum; British Library.[46] (Endangered Archives Project 466: completed.)

### North Africa

Binsbergen, Wim van. Historic Berber Culture[47] and Popular Islam in North Africa[48]
Includes articles on popular Islam and Khumiriyya in northwestern Tunisia.

### South Africa

Community Video Education Trust.[49]
Includes videos[50] of Muslim antiapartheid role of 1980s.

## General Resources

African Blue Books, 1821–1953[51]*
Includes full-text British colonial sources. Some reports cover matters to do with Islam.

African Newspapers[52]* (World Newspaper Archive)[53]
1800–1922 African newspapers. Those from, for example, Nigeria, Ghana, and Sierra Leone, carry various reports and articles on Islam in West Africa (a search by "Islam" gives 2,093 hits).

---

45 "The Manuscripts of the Riyadh Mosque of Lamu, Kenya," http://eap.bl.uk/database/overview_project.a4d?projID=EAP466;r=3753.
46 Anne Bang, Chr. Michelsen Institute, and National Museums of Kenya, Lamu Museum.
47 "Historic Berber Culture," http://www.shikanda.net/Berber/index.htm.
48 "Popular Islam in North Africa," http://www.shikanda.net/african_religion/islamfo.htm.
49 "Community Video Education Trust," http://www.cvet.org.za.
50 "And so the rally came to an end with thousands of Muslims resolved that they will not vote for apartheid," part of "Community Video Education Trust," http://www.cvet.org.za/displayvideo.php?vid=2D-F5-14.
51 "African Blue Books, 1821–1953," http://www.britishonlinearchives.co.uk/collection.php?cid=9781851172740.
52 "African Newspapers," http://www.readex.com/content/african-newspapers-1800-1922.
53 "World Newspaper Archive," http://www.readex.com/content/world-newspaper-archive.

Centre for Contemporary Islam[54] (University of Cape Town)

Publishes *Annual Review of Islam in South Africa*[55] (1998–2005 full text) and *Journal for Islamic Studies*, peer-reviewed, not online.

Center for the Study of Islam and Democracy[56] (Washington, D.C.)

"Non-profit organization, dedicated to studying Islamic and democratic political thought and merging them into a modern Islamic democratic discourse." Includes publications and resources.

Centre of Islamic and Middle Eastern Law[57] (School of Oriental and African Studies, London)

Includes texts and extracts on Islamic law from various published works.

Index Islamicus[58]* (Brill)

Citations to 240,000+ articles and books.

Institute for the Study of Islamic Thought in Africa[59] (Northwestern University)

"Collaborative interdisciplinary scholarship on the Islamic tradition of learning in Africa." Includes ISITA Working Paper Series.[60] Publishes *Islamic Africa*.[61]

Islam in Comparative Context: Online Resources[62] (Berkeley)

Chiefly links to resources useful in the classroom.

Islam in Contemporary Sub-Saharan Africa[63] (Library, African Studies Centre, Leiden University)

By Paul Schrijver, updated by Ursula Oberst. More than 4,900 records, last updated: January 2011. Includes some links to full text (some proprietary).

*Islamic Africa*[64]

Peer-reviewed, multidisciplinary journal. Incorporates *Sudanic Africa*, retaining its focus on historical sources, bibliographies, methodologies. Promotes interaction between scholars of Islam and Africa.

---

[54] "Centre for Contemporary Islam," http://www.cci.uct.ac.za.

[55] *Annual Review of Islam in South Africa*, http://www.cci.uct.ac.za/publications/aria.

[56] "Center for the Study of Islam and Democracy," https://www.csidonline.org.

[57] "Centre of Islamic and Middle Eastern Law," http://www.soas.ac.uk/cimel.

[58] "Index Islamicus," http://bibliographies.brillonline.com/browse/index-islamicus.

[59] "Institute for the Study of Islamic Thought in Africa," http://www.isita.northwestern.edu.

[60] "ISITA Working Paper Series," http://www.cics.northwestern.edu/programs/isita/workingpapers.html.

[61] *Islamic Africa*, http://islamicafricajournal.org.

[62] "Islam in Comparative Context: Online Resources," http://orias.berkeley.edu/Islam.html.

[63] "Islam in Contemporary Sub-Saharan Africa," http://www.africabib.org/islam.htm.

[64] *Islamic Africa*, http://islamicafricajournal.org.

Islamic Studies: Oxford Bibliographies Online[65]*
Subscription-only, select bibliography.

"La question islamique en Afrique Noire"[66]
Special issue of *Politique africaine* 4, 1981 (full-text open access from the publisher).

Sankoreʾ Institute of Islamic-African Studies International[67]
"Researching . . . the educational, political, cultural and religious heritage of Islamic Africa."

Sharia Debates in Africa[68] (Universität Bayreuth)
"International, comparative, multidisciplinary research project"; some full-text articles, theses, books, for example, *Sharia Implementation in Northern Nigeria 1999–2006: A Sourcebook,* edited by P. Ostien (Ibadan, 2007).

Slavery and Anti-Slavery: A Transnational Archive[69]* (Farmington Hills, Mich.: Gale, 2007–).
Includes a range of nineteenth-century books in French and English that treat Islam in Africa.

The Story of Africa—Islam[70] (BBC)
ca. 2001? Part of a series on African history: very short texts with audio recordings ("ram" files) on intellectual traditions; practices; North Africa/Ethiopia; Berbers; East Africa; West Africa.

*Sudanic Africa*[71] (Centre for Middle Eastern Studies, University of Bergen)
Historical sources of Sudanic belt. Some articles full text (1990–2005); merged with *Islamic Africa.*

---

65 "Islamic Studies: Oxford Bibliographies Online," http://www.oxfordbibliographies.com/browse?module_0=obo-9780195390155.
66 "La question islamique en Afrique Noire," http://www.politique-africaine.com/numeros/004_SOM.HTM.
67 "Sankoreʾ Institute of Islamic-African Studies International," http://siiasi.org.
68 "Sharia Debates in Africa," http://www.sharia-in-africa.net.
69 "Slavery and Anti-Slavery: A Transnational Archive," http://gdc.gale.com/products/slavery-and-anti-slavery-a-transnational-archive.
70 "The Story of Africa—Islam," http://www.bbc.co.uk/worldservice/africa/features/storyofafrica/index_section7.shtml.
71 *Sudanic Africa*, http://org.uib.no/smi/sa/sahome.html.

# Muslim Societies in West Africa: Historical and Contemporary Perspectives in Digital Form

*David Robinson*, MICHIGAN STATE UNIVERSITY

DOI: 10.5192/215409930501103

**Abstract**

*Over the past decade, Matrix, the Center for Digital Humanities and Social Sciences at Michigan State University, has developed digital galleries blending text, sound, and image to portray the history of islamization and the practice of Islam in West Africa with support from NSF, TICFIA, and the NEH. The featured areas have been Ghana (as a Muslim minority country), and Senegal (as a Muslim majority area), as well as Gambia and Mauritania. The emphasis has been on the diversity, tolerance, and pluralism of Islamic practice in historical and contemporary terms, on female and male practitioners, and on laypeople as well as clergy. We have used European archives, Arabic and* ajami *documents, interviews, and a range of other sources to tell stories and show practices. The portal for this material is www.aodl.org. This article outlines some of the galleries that we have built; others will be added over the next two years. The authors of the galleries are faculty at Indiana University, Michigan State, Harvard, Boston University, and James Madison University. The designer of the galleries has been Catherine Foley, Director of Digital Library and Archive Projects at MATRIX, and the author of "Developing Materials for a Digital Library Gallery" in this issue of* Islamic Africa.

*Islamic Africa,* VOL. 5, NO. 1, 2014. ISSN 2154-0993.  www.islamicafricajournal.org

### *Introduction*

As the readers of this journal know well, West Africa has included Muslim societies and practices for over a thousand years. Parts of the region have become majority Muslim over the last few centuries. Some have adopted Arabic as their primary written and spoken language, while others have adapted the Arabic script to writing, reading, and reciting their own first languages. Most practice the faith with understanding and devotion. But these facts and sequences are little understood beyond the practitioners themselves and a few academics scattered across the world. If observers think of West Africa and Islam today, they are more likely to consider distortions of the faith, such as the Boko Haram movement in Nigeria or the Al-Qaeda offshoots exploiting the grievances of Tuareg and Arabs in Mali.

At Matrix, the Center for Digital Humanities and Social Sciences based at Michigan State University, we have sought over the last fifteen years to develop projects that highlight Islamic practice in West Africa. We have emphasized its adaptation, originality, and modernity, and the comfort which practitioners find alongside Christians, secularists, and persons of other persuasions. We have implemented this vision mainly through digital libraries organized by scholars of West Africa at Michigan State, Indiana, and other institutions. These libraries are designed for researchers, teachers, and students of Africa and Islam, and for the constantly changing processes of teaching and learning. We have placed these libraries at a portal, the Africa Online Digital Library, accessible at www.aodl.org. In these essays for *Islamic Africa* we seek to show some of what we have achieved, some of its potential for various audiences, and the processes and problems we have encountered along the way.

In my own work in trying to understand the processes of becoming Muslim in sub-Saharan Africa, I have approached the subject in two complementary, overlapping, and clumsy ways: the Islamization of Africa, and the Africanization of Islam.[1] The first is akin to the more traditional approach which experts on Islam in sub-Saharan Africa have used: finding the routes, the agents, and the societies where Islam was first practiced and from which it expanded. Insiders and outsiders considered certain societies to be Muslim, on the whole, and others to be "pagan." The "frontier" between these two groups was somewhere between the Sahel and the for-

[1] See David Robinson, *Muslim Societies in African History* (Cambridge University Press, 2004), especially chapters 3 and 4.

est regions to the south. The spread of Islam continued through the colonial and independence periods, and has at least partially obscured this frontier.

The second approach is more novel, and features the appropriation of Islamic practices to local customs, seasons, and communities. This Africanization of Islam is *not* the same as the diminishment or compromising of the faith, as some Islamicists and Islamic purists would have us believe, and it has no relationship to the pejorative formulation of *Islam noir* that the French used through much of the twentieth century. Rather, this process is similar to the ones that Christianity and other faiths have undergone, as they have spread from their birth regions and taken root around the world. Both Africanization and Islamization can of course be applied to all of sub-Saharan Africa, and not just West Africa.

One of the best and oldest examples of the Africanization of Islam is the "Suwarian" tradition which Ivor Wilks of Northwestern University elaborated in many works.[2] This practice, which goes back some 500 years, takes its name from a scholar of the middle Niger region, al-hajj Salim Suwari (fl. ca. 1500), who developed a rationale for Muslims merchants living in non-Muslim societies. His teachings passed on orally, across the generations and centuries, and became especially important among merchants who emigrated to the southern forest zones as part of the expansion of the Mali Empire (fl. 1300–1500). These merchants or *juula* constituted important religious minorities among the traditional practitioners of the societies of today's southern Ghana and Côte d'Ivoire. They had their own mosques and systems of socialization and education, and fulfilled all the obligations of the faith. In that they were no different from Muslims anywhere in the globe. But they made no effort to change the practices of the "pagans" who lived around them; they thought that God would bring these people to Islam in his own time. They cooperated to some extent with the chiefly estates that dominated the southern Akan areas, and often provided amulets with Qurʾanic verses in them—a way of adding "Muslim power" to the armament that individuals sought in their daily lives. In the historical case we know best, the Asante Empire of the nineteenth century, these *juula* sometimes found themselves in compromising situations—between their faith and the obligations placed on them by the local authorities. But the point here is the originality and practical-

[2] For a recent formulation of the Suwarian tradition by Wilks, see his chapter in *A History of Islam in Africa*, ed. Nehemia Levtzion and Randall Pouwels (Ohio University Press, 2000). For my summary of this, see Robinson, *Muslim Societies*, especially chapters 4 and 9.

ity of the theology which allowed Muslim minorities to function within a non-Muslim framework. Similar rationales undoubtedly existed across the Islamic frontiers the world over.

Alongside the spread of Islam and Islamic practices has come the spread of various forms of modernity, set in motion by the increasing domination of the West over the last 200 or more years. Some of this hegemony took the form of colonial rule by European powers that formed the present boundaries of Africa and many of its institutions in the twentieth century. African territories became independent at various times in the mid-twentieth century, but the Western influence, and the imperatives of modernity, persisted and persist in all sorts of ways. Most African countries are poor, most African governments and institutions are weak, and the disparities within countries between rich and poor, between rulers and subjects, are great. In the midst of all this, African societies have found ways to adopt modernity, modify long traditions of adaptation, and remain authentic in the process. Muslims have been prominent in this process, in their own institutions and in collaboration with Africans of other faiths and persuasions.

Over the last decade Africanists at Indiana and Michigan State universities, working under the leadership of Matrix, the Center for Digital Humanities and Social Sciences, have used their work on Muslim societies in West Africa to highlight these themes of Africanization and modernization. They have focused on Senegambia and Ghana, two areas that have very different configurations of religious practice but demonstrate positive relations between Muslims, other practitioners, and the state. Senegambia is a majority Muslim area, in the two countries that share that space: Francophone Senegal and Anglophone Gambia. Ghana has a Muslim minority, one that has often been regarded as "traditional" and "anti-modern," but our work shows how misplaced these stereotypes are. Together Senegambia and Ghana show the originality, dynamism, and importance of Islam in West Africa, and an appropriate subject for this issue of *Islamic Africa*. The work of these specialists has been formulated into digital galleries for researchers, students, and teachers of Africa, Islam, and religion, and often contain references and links to archival and other resources which users can pursue on their own. Since many of our galleries contain excerpts from interviews and transcripts, they can also be used for learning African languages. The ones we have constructed, and are adding to, can be found at the above-mentioned portal, www.aodl.org, a site which Matrix developed fifteen years ago. I will be writing about some of them in the rest of this presentation.

The titles of the various grants of external support show how we have conceived the work of understanding and showcasing Muslim societies in Senegambia and Ghana. The first grant, which came from TICFIA, the Technological Innovation and Cooperation for Foreign Information Access program of the U.S. Department of Education,[3] was entitled "Diversity and Tolerance in the Islam of West Africa: Creating Online Resources of Peaceful Muslim Practice in Senegal and Ghana." It provided funds from 2005 to 2009 and also involved collaborators at Harvard and James Madison universities. The second and third grants come from the NEH Collaborative Research grant program and featured MSU and Indiana. "Pluralism and Adaptation in the Islamic Practice of Senegal and Ghana" lasted from 2008 to 2011. The current grant, "Islam and Modernity: Alternatives in Contemporary Senegambia and Ghana," will go until 2015.[4]

In all of this work we have sought to construct galleries which demonstrate three themes: first, the Africanization of Islam and the adaptation of the faith to the cultures and realities of West Africa; second, the various modernities of Islamic practice in the region; and third, the pluralism of religious practice, both within the Muslim communities and in their relations to persons of other faiths and secular entities. We have identified scholars with competence on the Muslim societies of the region, experience in working with the written, oral, and visual documentation, and an interest in the themes of Africanization, modernization, and pluralism—and a commitment to reaching new and old audiences about Africa and Islam.

## *Historiography and Older Cases*

The older historiography about Islamization in West Africa follows the trajectory cited above, and culminates with militant jihads, associated in particular with the Fulbe or Fulani ethnic group, and the Islamic states that

[3] TICFIA no longer exists, a victim of the savage budget cutting of a few years ago.

[4] A related project, funded by the British Library's Endangered Archives program, has digitized civil, police, and criminal records dating from the 1820s held in the Court Record collections of the Department of State for Justice in Banjul, The Gambia. This project was carried out in 2010–11 by Walter Hawthorne and Bala Saho of MSU in cooperation with the National Records Services (NRS) of The Gambia and MATRIX's head of digitization at the time, Scott Pennington. No materials have yet been made available to the public online, but the digitizing has been carried out to the exacting standards of the Endangered Archives program.

they created in the eighteenth and nineteenth centuries.[5] It assumes that the jihads were a capstone to a progression of Islam to majority and dominant status in the West African Sahel, the belt extending from Senegal in the west to Nigeria, Cameroon, and Chad in the east. The jihad that was the most famous and far-reaching was the one led by Uthman dan Fodio in Hausaland, the core of today's northern Nigeria, in the early nineteenth century. It resulted in the creation of the Sokoto Caliphate, a regime that accomplished a great deal to spread the faith, in breadth and depth, partly through a vast literature of interpretation and pedagogy written by its leaders in the midst of their revolutionary activities.[6]

The last of these movements, in chronological terms, was the one led by Umar Tall, a Senegalese Muslim who made the pilgrimage (1828–30), was commissioned to spread allegiance to a new Sufi order, the Tijaniyya, and visited the other jihadic states on his return from Mecca. From 1852 until his death in 1864, al-hajj Umar, as he is commonly known, led a jihad against the Mandinka and especially Bamana states of the upper and middle Niger area. He built an army around Senegambian Muslims to conquer large areas of today's Mali. For a brief moment he created a regime in the Western Sudan which resembled—in extent—the Sokoto Caliphate in the Central Sudan.[7]

One of our galleries challenges this assumption of progressive Islamization through militant jihad, especially in reference to the work of Umar. It makes the case that militant and military movements often failed to spread the faith, gave a negative reputation to the vision of the Islamic state, and unintentionally opened the way to a more profound Islamization,

[5] The leading interpreter was John Spencer Trimingham, a former missionary and Arabist who wrote a number of volumes on Islam in sub-Saharan Africa in the mid-twentieth century. His most relevant works for West Africa were *Islam in West Africa* (Oxford University Press, 1959) and *A History of Islam in West Africa* (Oxford University Press, 1962).

[6] The most thorough work on the foundations of this movement and regime is still D. Murray Last, *The Sokoto Caliphate* (New York: Humanities, 1967). For a recent reflection on the process, see his article "Contradictions in Creating a Jihadi Capital: Sokoto and Its Legacy in the Nineteenth Century," in the *African Studies Review* 56, no. 2 (September 2013).

[7] The most complete account of Umar's jihad is my *Holy War of Umar Tall: The Western Sudan in the Mid-Nineteenth Century* (Oxford University Press, 1985). The fullest account of efforts by his son and successor, Ahmad al-Kabir, to hold together the vast Umarian conquests is John Hanson, *Migration, Jihad and Muslim Authority in West Africa: The Futanke Colonies in Karta* (Indiana University Press, 1996). For a collection of documents and translations about Ahmad's reign, see John Hanson and David Robinson, *After the Jihad: The Reign of Ahmad al-Kabir in the Western Sudan* (Michigan State University Press, 1991).

through Sufi movements in recent times. To make this point I built a gallery, "Failed Islamic States," primarily around the experience of Umar (ca. 1797–1864) and his oldest son and successor, Ahmad al-Kabir (reigned 1864–93), and their inability to realize an Islamic state or to spread the faith in the ways that the Sokoto regime accomplished to a significant degree. Umar was consumed by the military challenge of defeating powerful Bamana armies, a process that he formulated as the "destruction of paganism." Ahmad was preoccupied by a more or less constant insurgency of the same Bamana societies but also by rebellions from his own brothers, who did not accept his right to the succession. I use the formulation of *fitna*, the term for "civil war" used by scholars for the struggles of the faith after the death of the Prophet, to capture the strife among the brothers. The result was not only that Islam did not spread. It was often considered by the Bamana to be an imperial imposition by the Senegambian Muslims who dominated the Umarian legions. The widespread Islamization of the Bamana and other Mande peoples of today's Mali came from other sources, often Sufi, and it happened to a great extent under colonial rule.

I also document a movement that operated briefly in northwestern Senegal in the 1860s and 1870s, and went by the name of Madiyanke. The Madiyankoobe, or "those of the Mahdi," were led by sons of a cleric who had taken the title of Mahdi, the one who comes to lead the faithful at the end of time, and who developed a sharp critique of the "Islamic regime" that had been created in his homeland of Futa Toro in the late eighteenth century.[8] The sons reacted to a devastating cholera epidemic that gripped Senegambia in 1868–69, and took it as God's sign of disfavor with the existing regimes and their growing ties to the French in Saint-Louis. They attracted a substantial following amid the general distress and became the dominant force in western Futa and the Wolof states of Jolof, Cayor, and Walo. They did little to spread the faith, but they delivered a severe and enduring judgment on the regimes and the ruling classes of their day. The French and the Wolof armies, led in particular by Lat Dior of Cayor, finally dealt a devastating defeat to the Madiyanke forces in 1875, killed most of the leaders, and dispersed the survivors. The Madiyanke failure again opened the way for the more peaceful practices that dominate the Senegambian scene today. See this gallery of the Umarian and Madiyanke

[8] For a fuller treatment, see David Robinson, *Chiefs and Clerics: Abdul Bokar Kan and the History of Futa Toro, 1853–1891* (Oxford: Clarendon Press, 1975), chapters 4 and 5.

efforts based on archives, interviews, and images, at www.aodl.org/islamicpluralism/failedislamicstates/.

This gallery about failure serves as an introduction to the more peaceful initiatives that have spread the faith and demonstrate the themes of Africanization, adaptation, modernization, and pluralism. One example of the adaptation of Islam to West African realities comes in the form of *ajami* literatures developed within the "Islamic" languages and cultures of the region. *Ajami* is the Arabic word for non-Arabic or foreign. It has come to be applied to the adaptation of the Arabic script for writing the local languages.[9] This practice, going back at least 300 years in West Africa, developed in Kanuri, Hausa, Fulbe, Wolof, and various Mande societies. It may well have started in the ways in which Qurʾanic scholars taught the scripture in local languages to succeeding generations. With the expansion of Islam, Muslim leaders developed literatures of *ajami* for recitation to the illiterate majorities of their societies, including women and slaves. The best-known examples of this come from the Sokoto Caliphate of northern Nigeria, and are known especially from the work of Jean Boyd and Beverly Mack.[10] The best-known practitioner was Nana Asmau, the daughter of the founder of the Sokoto regime, Uthman dan Fodio. She lived through much of the nineteenth century, beginning with the jihad that established the regime, and became a vital part of the outreach and pedagogy which helped to root the practice of Islam in the small villages and rural areas around Sokoto.

An example of this *ajami* composition, designed for recitation, is a poem written in Fulfulde and Hausa in which Uthman sought to compare his accomplishments to those of Muhammad the Prophet, and thereby encourage participation in the jihad and Islamic state. Nana Asmau used it as she sought to deepen the understanding of Islamic practice among women, children, slaves, and others who had no access to the written word. In

---

[9] The best known of these literatures is Swahili, and there is considerable Swahili literature published in Arabic and Roman script. See Robinson, *Muslim Societies*, chapters 3 and 4.

[10] Jean Boyd, *The Caliph's Sister* (London: Cass, 1989), and Jean Boyd and Beverly Mack, *One Woman's Jihad: Nana Asmaʾu, Scholar and Scribe* (Indiana University Press, 2000). Boyd and Mack also collaborated on a monumental exposition of the literature written and recited by Nana Asmau, including Hausa reproductions and transcriptions, in *The Collected Works of Nana Asmaʾu, 1793–1864* (Michigan State University Press, 1997). The other well-known example comes from Futa Jalon and especially the province and town of Labe, and has been examined by Alfa Ibrahima Sow in a number of works.

English we can call it "The Attributes of the Shaikh." A partial selection follows:

> In the name of God, the Beneficent, the Merciful; may God bless the noble Prophet.
>
> I give thanks to God for the generosity he showed me,
> I give praise to Him, the Generous One.
> I say "Peace be upon our prophet."
> Know that I have [obtained] many of his characteristics. . . .
> Know that he bore with the troubles of the people,
> Likewise am I known for this and for loving peace.
> Indeed, he never angered anyone;
> For this too have people known me and for mercy.
> After summoning people to the religion he made the *hijra*,
> When I made mine it cost me great effort.
> At that place where the enemies came out
> As [they failed] against him so also against me did they fail.
> By making the *hijra* he was indeed saved [from them],
> I did the same and the same has been repeated.
> He made it at the beginning of the sixth decade [of his life],
> Of a truth, mine was indeed [made at] the same [time]. . . .
> No sooner had he made the *hijra* than he waged the *jihad*;
> Likewise did I, keeping the pattern. . . .[11]

### *Contemporary Cases*

We have not done any galleries with the Sokoto material or Nigeria, but we have explored similar themes in Senegambia. Fallou Ngom, a linguist at Boston University, has been one of the pioneers in exploring the *ajami* literatures of more recent times, and particularly in reference to Wolof, the dominant language of Senegambia. The written and recited Wolof is called Wolofal, and Ngom has taken works by Murid scholar-poets and showed

---

[11] The first published example that I have found of this poem is from an English translation of the Hausa poem by Uthman, entitled "Sifofin Shehu" and made by R. A. Adeleye and I. A. Mukoshy in the *Research Bulletin* of the Center of Arabic Documentation (Ibadan), vol. 2, no. 1 (January 1966): 26–27. Douglas Smith and I reprinted this in *Sources of the African Past* (Heinemann, 1979), 140.

the ways in which they celebrated Islamic themes in their work. Amadu Bamba Mbacke, founder of the important Sufi order that is the Muridiyya, did not write in Wolofal himself, but he preached eloquently in the Wolof language and blessed the efforts of his collaborators to create a written repository that would deepen and broaden the practice for the faithful. For him, why should Wolof not be as much a language of inspiration and devotion as Arabic? Ngom's gallery features the work of Serigne Ndame Diop, a grandson of one of Bamba's close disciples and an inhabitant of Diourbel. Diourbel is an important Murid center and the place where Bamba got his first measure of freedom from the French in 1912, even though he was still essentially under house arrest. Serigne Ndame's main document here is called "Tolerance in Muridiyya Teachings," and you can choose to study the Wolofal script, listen to the recitation in Wolof, or read the transcription in Wolof, English, or French. Look for Ngom's gallery at www.islamictolerance/ajami.

The Muridiyya itself is an example of adaptation, modernization, and pluralism. Founded by stages in the late nineteenth century by Amadu Bamba (ca. 1853–1927), it was shaped by the failure of ambitious efforts to create Islamic states in the region (see my gallery, "Failed Islamic States"), the availability of peaceful and largely Sufi alternatives, and the growing power of the French. By 1900 Senegal was a French colony and the key territory within the archipelago called French West Africa, with a "federal" capital at the port city of Dakar. Bamba never espoused a militant or military jihad or the intention to create an Islamic state, but he could not persuade the colonial authorities of his peaceful intentions and endured three multiyear exiles at their hands. The most famous was the first, to Gabon from 1895 to 1902, and has resulted in a tremendous outpouring of poetry and art by Bamba and his supporters. It has created an image of "spiritual resistance" to colonial rule. In 1912 Bamba was finally released from his third exile and allowed to live out the rest of his life (1912–27) in Diourbel, in his home province of Baol about 100 miles east of Dakar.

Bamba was fundamentally about creating "Muslim space" within the colonial regime and developing a pedagogy for teaching Islamic practice in a new age. He and his contemporaries were so successful that Murid Muslims have spread throughout Senegambia, Africa, Europe, North America, and the world. We show some dimensions of this on our website, "Passport to Paradise," which is part of an exhibit which Al and Polly Nooter Roberts developed about ten years ago at UCLA. See www.aodl.org/westafrica/passport/php. Many of the images in the collection are glass paintings. Examine the one entitled *Amadu Bamba Praying on the Water*, which recalls, in the minds of the Murid faithful, the first exile of the Murid founder. Based on Bamba's accounts, this painting reflects the founder's ability to create "Muslim space" wherever he found himself. The French boat transporting him to Gabon was "hostile" colonial territory. Accordingly Bamba unfurled his mat on the ocean and conducted his prayers, in spite of the threatening sharks. He amazed the captain, administrator, and priest gazing down from the deck of the ship. Artists such as this painter have taken the Murid story and put it into images that become resources for practitioners of the faith, wherever they may be.[12]

An even more explicit development of Islam for contemporary times comes from Ghana in the form of the Ahmadiyya. This order developed in British India in the late nineteenth century under the leadership of Ghulam Ahmad, who claimed to be the messiah or prophet renewing the vision embodied in Muhammad. As one can imagine, his movement was controversial from the beginning, and is often regarded as heresy by other Muslims. Its practice, however, conforms to Islamic norms and places a special emphasis on modernity. It spread quickly, through agents who were not unlike Christian missionaries, to other parts of the British Empire. One of its most successful implantations started in the 1920s in the colony of the Gold Coast, today's Ghana. The first Ahmadis were Indians but they gave way soon to Ghanaian leadership. They were very successful in attracting Muslims and new converts to their mosques, schools, and other institutions, first in the southern region and then in most parts of the colony and country. They endured the critiques of many in the traditional Muslim community, but they equipped their faithful for living in Ghana in the twentieth century and related well to Christian and secular communities. They were devoted practitioners of Islam and accustomed to a plural religious universe at the same time. The leading interpreter of Ahmadi history in Ghana, John Hanson of Indiana, will be developing a gallery for our collection.[13] He will be dealing with all of our themes, but with an additional

[12] An active participant in our work is Cheikh Anta Babou of the University of Pennsylvania, author of the leading interpretation of the Murid founder's life (*Fighting the Greater Jihad* [Ohio University Press, 2008]) and a likely future contributor to our site. He was also the very first Africanist to be interviewed in the podcasts established by Peter Alegi and Peter Limb of Michigan State. He talked about Bamba and the Murids at afripod.aodl.org/2008/01/africa-past-present/.

[13] See his article "Jihad and the Ahmadiyya Community: Non-Violent Efforts to Promote Islam in the Contemporary World," *Nova Religio*, 2007.

twist: the adaptation of a version of Islam developed in British India to the realities of an African colony and then an independent state.

Most of the more "traditional" Muslims of Ghana are not vocal Islamists but people with a long history of "embedment" in the local societies, especially those of the northern provinces which have a long history of practice. Some of the leaders in the key towns can be found in a gallery prepared by Emmanuel Akyeampong of Harvard and built around extensive interviews. You can follow this at www.aodl.org/islamictolerance/asantehistory.

You may wish to start with the material on Salaga, long designated by the Asante Empire as the center for trade with the north, a kind of transit center where Hausa and other merchants from the Sahel met their counterparts from the south. Like so many places in Ghana, it was multilingual—Guan, Gur languages, Twi, and Hausa were all spoken, and it was a place for scholarship and libraries of manuscripts. Look at the interview with the paramount chief of Gonja province, Kwembiwura Alhaji Ibrahim Haruna, for an extensive narrative of the complex history of Salaga, the northern centers, and the leading Muslim families. Haruna shows how the older commercial and religious practices have been modified over time.

Most of what we've mentioned so far features Muslim leaders and their choices. This is not surprising, since the leaders are usually clerics, literate in Arabic and local languages, and accustomed to speaking and writing about Islam. But they are only a small minority of the Muslim population. Through the work of Gracia Clark of Indiana, and her research in the principal marketplace of Ghana's second city, Kumasi, we see the practices of lay women and men engaged at various points in the local economy. She approached her work primarily through interviews, not written documents, and features video recorded interviews on her three planned web galleries.

Her first gallery, "Everyday Islam in Kumasi: Devout Lay Men and Women in Daily Life," can be seen at www.aodl/isalmictolerance/kumasi. More than twenty interviews in English show how merchants, craft workers, teachers, and students practice their faith, the impact that it has on their daily lives, and the way they understand virtue and the good life. Members of women's study groups at several mosques and a men's street salon or daily discussion group volunteered to participate. They were partially motivated by an interest in correcting current stereotypes about Islam and their own practice of it. Photos of typical scenes and short explanations of the history of trade and Islam in Kumasi complement the interviews. Have a look at Clark's interview with Rukaya Usman. She tells of her family origins in Burkina Faso, her childhood years in Liberia as a cocoa laborer and waitress, and her return to Kumasi to take care of her father. She considered working as a seamstress, after some years as an apprentice, but settled on buying and selling local produce. Her strong Muslim identity does not preclude good relations with the more numerous Christian families in her neighborhood.

Clark's second web gallery will expand on these personal interpretations of Muslim concepts such as peace, submission, modesty, honesty, and mutual responsibility, as these appear in daily life experiences at home and at work. Video recorded interviews are again featured, including many in local languages (principally Twi, Hausa, and Dagbani) to facilitate access by the participating communities and to foster advanced language skills among nonnative speakers. Each will be synchronized with text translations into English and transcriptions in the local languages as these become available. The majority of the participants spoke from their personal experiences in marriage, home life, business, and migration. More extensive interviews with local teachers and informal religious leaders address at greater length questions of gender and family relations, Arab influence, jihad, and the roots of terrorism. Several elders record versions of the history of the Kumasi Islamic community.

This gallery presents short video clips first, but enables the interested reader to download digital files of entire interviews. The alert student can learn much from the topics selected and emphasized, from their sequence or linkages within each narrative and from nonverbal signals. The participants merge honesty and other Islamic virtues as practiced by themselves and others in the contexts of family, work, and migration. Adherence to these virtues is no sacrifice in the long run, since it leads to more stable and profitable relationships that benefit the devout.

Clark's third gallery will focus on the public expression of Islam in Kumasi, drawing on extensive video documentation of festivals and religious holidays. At the end of Ramadan, a historic parade from the main mosque to the Zongo chief's palace enables wide recognition of the varied and cross-cutting identities that make up the Zongo or foreign/Islamic community. Groups march in colorful uniforms representing ethnic affiliations, nations of origin, loyalties to distinct schools or brotherhoods, modern political parties, and prominent occupations associated with Muslim immigrants, like butchers and cattle traders. It demonstrates the regional integration focused on Kumasi with representatives of chiefs from neighboring countries, although fewer than in the past. The march itself has become a point of controversy between local Sufi interpreters of the Qurʾan and the new orthodoxy emanating from Saudi Arabia. Celebrations of smaller festivals already recorded show how these differ between the two trends, who have now established separate Friday mosques throughout Kumasi.

Some galleries deal in greater depth with the relations of Muslim and Christian communities in Ghana and Senegambia. Emmanuel Akyeampong of Harvard and David Owusu-Ansah of James Madison University explore ties between Muslims and Christians in Ghana, and again feature the city of Kumasi, once the proud capital of the Asante Empire and site of an important "Suwarian" merchant community that exercised considerable influence at the court. The empire held off British armies, as well as Christian missionaries, for most of the nineteenth century. In the twentieth century, however, and with the installation of British rule of the Gold Coast and a more circumscribed role for Asante and its ruler within a colonial framework, Christianity began to spread, especially after the conversion to Anglican Christianity of the exiled king Prempeh. In numbers and influence Christianity soon overtook the older Muslim minorities of southern Ghana and became a main avenue of modernization. Owusu Ansah's gallery is available at www.aodl.org/islamictolerance/seculareducation.

Pluralism emerges from all of these Ghanaian materials, as well as the adaptations of Muslims of very different stripes to a plural universe. I have used the word "pluralism" in the title of my gallery on the Muslims, Christians, secularists, and French administrators in Saint-Louis, an old town at the mouth of the Senegal River. Saint-Louis was the capital of French commercial and military operations in the region long before it became the capital of two colonial territories, Senegal and Mauritania, around 1900. At independence in 1960, the town ceded the capital of independent Senegal to Dakar, and to Nouakchott for Mauritania. But in the nineteenth century Saint-Louis was the hub of French expansion and home to many communities. They included the Catholic Church and its missionaries, who often protested that the colonial administration favored the Muslims and even the operations of the Masons, who harbored a strong anti-Catholic and antireligious bias under the Third Republic in France. The Islamic community grew steadily, and at some point in the nineteenth century Saint-Louis became a majority Muslim town. Muslims, Catholics, Masons, secularists, and administrators found ways to get along in the concentrated confines of the town, and to create a tradition of pluralism and understanding. You can follow this in my gallery at www.aodl.org/islamictolerance/saintlouis.

Look at three items in particular. In the "Documents" section, consult the petition of 1843, written in Arabic and translated into French, for the creation of a Muslim Tribunal for the adjudication of issues involving the local community of the faithful. The court was finally created in 1857, by Governor Leon Louis Cesar Faidherbe, who sought to enlist local Muslims in support of his expansion and other causes.[14] Note the varying degrees of fluency in writing Arabic among the signatories. Then look at the piece by one of the leading Muslims of Saint-Louis, Bu El Mogdad Seck, as he explains his rationale in 1860 for making the pilgrimage to Mecca with colonial government support. Part of his reasoning is to combat the prestige of al-hajj Umar, pilgrim, Tijaniyya leader, and jihad leader, and a person who had strong influence in Senegal at that time. I've already discussed the Umarian jihad in the gallery "Failed Islamic States."

Then look at Bu El Mogdad's picture in the "Image" section. It is quite formal, in dress robe with French medals conspicuously pinned on his chest. The photo, obviously posed and professionally done, suggests how prestigious and well-educated Muslims were able to work within and indeed serve the French administration as it expanded into Senegal and what later became French West Africa. Bu El Mogdad is dressed in a "boubou," and his prayer beads hang around his neck. In his hand is a document, an indication of his literacy. He often translated into and from Arabic—letters between the colonial administration and the clerics and chiefs of the interior, just as he embarked on diplomatic missions to persuade these Senegalese that good Muslims could live in harmony with the French and even come under their control. He was a *hajj*, a pilgrim, but he could also wear the medals which his superiors had awarded him. The image "says" much of what the French regime of the late nineteenth century was trying to say about the compatibility of a secular administration and Muslim identity.

One of the most prestigious Muslim leaders who worked with the administration in Saint-Louis and helped frame the French conquest of Mauritania was Sidiyya Baba. I am currently developing a gallery about his collaboration and modernization, which date from about 1900 to his death in 1924. This pattern was perpetuated by his sons and disciples through the time of independence and the creation of the Republique Islamique de

[14] For the only extant study of the Muslim Tribunal of Saint-Louis, see the article of Ghislaine Lydon, "Obtaining Freedom at the Muslim Tribunal," in *Muslim Family Law in Sub-Saharan Africa: Colonial Legacies and Post-Colonial Challenges*, eds. Richard Roberts, Shamil Jeppie, and Ebrahim Ibrahim (Amsterdam University Press, 2009).

la Mauritanie (RIM).[15] Baba was a full partner with the French in the planning and execution of conquering Mauritania and making it the eighth territory within their West Africa federation in the early twentieth century. He worked closely with Xavier Coppolani, who framed the initiative as "pacification." After Coppolani's assassination in 1905, Baba continued the collaboration with Henri Gouraud, who completed much of the conquest in 1908–9. He encouraged the French military to use his base of Butilimit for telegraph services, training camelry units, and key logistics and supply.

In January 1903, just as the "pacification" plan of Coppolani was about to be launched, Sidiyya Baba composed and circulated a *fatwa* of immense utility to justify the French advance into Muslim territory north of the river. Drawing on the jurist Khalil ibn Ishaq and other sources with impeccable credentials, and noting that the Muslims of the eastern Maghrib were already living under French rule, Baba declared that the military jihad of resistance would only bring exhaustion to Muslim societies. It was especially to be rejected when Muslims were in a situation of weakness:

> It is evident that the obligation [to wage] holy war disappears in the face of the inability to accomplish it. . . . The inability of this land [of Muslims] to fight against the force of the Christians is obvious. Any sane man who hears and sees is aware of the absence of unity among Muslims, the absence of a public treasury necessary for any action, and the inferiority of their weapons in comparison to those of the Christians. . . . [There is also no obligation] to emigrate, *en masse* or in part, from the territory conquered by the "infidel," because of poverty as well as the absence of destinations where the necessary security and resources exist.

Baba did not stop there. He noted that the French had demonstrated that they would not interfere with the practice of the faith; indeed, that they would give positive support to the institutions of worship, education, and law. Their rule promised an end to the conditions of anarchy, *fitna*, which had plagued the societies of northwest Africa, and the beginning of conditions of peace and stability which would enable Islam to consolidate its position:

---

[15] In anticipation of the creation of this new gallery, see Robinson, *Paths of Accommodation* (Ohio University Press, 2000), chapter 9. It summarizes the relations of Baba with the French, including the creation of colonial Mauritania and the custodianship of Amadu Bamba in the second exile.

> It must be said, in addition, that the conduct of the Christians . . . [is what is required by Islam]. They not only do not oppose the exercise of religion, they also provide positive support in the construction of mosques, appointment of *qadis* and provision of a good organizational structure.

The French could not have asked for a more fulsome endorsement of conquest and colonial rule.

Baba pushed the limits of cooperation with the "infidel," and endured serious criticism from Muslim authorities who were engaged in resistance with some support from the court of Morocco. For them Mauritania was clearly part of the *Dar al-Islam* (abode of Islam) and could not accept the domination of non-Muslims. The Sidiyya family endured this critique throughout Baba's life and beyond, but this did not prevent them from working closely with the French even after Mauritanian independence in 1960. This portrayal will be featured in the gallery which I am preparing now as part of the new NEH grant.

Baba also played a role in the formulation of *Islam noir*, the designation that the French used for distinguishing the "inferior" Islamic practice of black Muslims in their West African federation from the Moors and "heartland" practitioners of the faith. *Islam noir* represented the racism of both Moors and French, and was part of a general diminishment of the civilization of sub-Saharan Africa in relation to the West. It was captured in the decision of the colonial authorities of Senegal to "entrust" Amadu Bamba to Baba during his second exile (1903–7); surely, they reasoned, a "black" Muslim would submit to the superior understanding of a "white" Moorish cleric. This submission did not happen and Bamba inaugurated the Muridiyya precisely during this exile. But the failure of the experiment did not change the attitudes of superiority of either the Moors or the French. The colonial authorities used *Islam noir* to limit the exposure of West Africans to other Muslims, not least in the pilgrimage to Mecca just as it became increasingly practiced in the twentieth century. It was only in the period of decolonization after World War II that the barriers were broken, as some West Africans began to study in Egypt and bring back different, more "modern" views of the faith.[16]

Less spectacular and less well known than Baba and Bamba, but equally influential among the faithful, was a Sufi brotherhood called the Buh Kunta,

---

[16] Louis Brenner, in *Controlling Knowledge: Religion, Power and Schooling in a West African Muslim Society* (Indiana University Press, 2001), deals with this issue in French Soudan/Mali. See also Robinson, *Paths of Accommodation.*

a branch of the larger entity called the Qadiriyya. Buh Kunta, a member of the prestigious Kunta family, established a multiethnic and multinational community in the area that was rapidly becoming colonial Senegal during the latter part of the nineteenth century. Many of his followers were Bamana, Soninke, Mandinka, and Mossi from the regions to the east who came to cultivate peanuts or work on colonial labor projects. Some of them were former slaves or indentured servants who found a welcome, and an equality that they did not enjoy in the larger society, within the Buh Kunta community. From their center in Ndiassane not far from Thiès, Buh Kunta and his successors developed their own institutions of education, transmission of knowledge, worship, and pilgrimage. Many family members and some disciples have received their religious education in Mauritania. Although Wolof is the lingua franca in Ndiassane, many speak Bamana and serve as liaisons with contemporary disciples in Mali. Conspicuous in the Buh Kunta community is the prominent involvement of women, some of whom have received the title of "shaykh." Maria Grosz-Ngaté, an anthropologist at Indiana University, has built this gallery with interviews, documents, and photographs, and it can be found at www.aodl.org/islamictolerance/ndiassane.

Court records are often an excellent source for exploring religious practices and gender relations, especially within colonial societies. We are pursuing Africanization and modernity through records of Islamic courts. Walter Hawthorne and Bala Sako are following these themes in a court in Banjul, Gambia. The Muslims of Banjul, like those of Saint-Louis, Senegal, demanded the establishment of a Muslim court in addition to the secular colonial jurisdictions, and in 1905 the British complied. Since then the court has produced thousands of court cases on matrimonial and property rights issues—matters of conflict resolution and management. The transcripts reveal detailed information about challenges faced by women within the household and other social relationships. The majority of these documents are in Arabic; a few were translated into English at the time of trial. They are important for understanding social history and how Muslim women and men coped with the realities of modernity and colonial rule and shaped the court.[17] They have been largely ignored by scholars of Senegambia.

[17] See Ghislaine Lydon's article cited in note 14, and her attention to the use which women made of the Muslim Tribunal of Saint-Louis, in Roberts et al., eds. *Muslim Family Law*. See also her book *On Trans-Saharan Trails* (Cambridge, 2009), and the work of Richard Roberts, *Litigants and Households* (Heinemann, 2005).

## *Epilogue*

We have a recent example of saving the precious West African heritage of a diverse, rich, and pluralistic Islamic practice—next door to Senegambia. In the last three years the nation of Mali has come under severe challenge. Initially it came from Tuareg and Arab citizens in the northern part of the country who have never been happy with a regime dominated by the Bamana, Bamako, and the south. Their challenge had the same overtones as the racial divisions expressed in *Islam noir* and the conflict between Moors and "blacks" in Mauritania and Senegal. But this challenge was quickly overtaken by radical Islamists affiliated with Al-Qaeda and armed with heavy weapons looted from Libya. These Islamists soon took control of the northern areas of the country and the towns of Kidal, Gao, and especially Timbuktu. In addition to their violence they dismissed the heritage of diversity, pluralism, and tolerance of the Malian majority in favor of their contorted visions of Islam. They destroyed the tombs of the Sufi saints around Timbuktu and threatened the rich heritage of Arabic manuscripts housed in private collections and the Centre Ahmed Baba of the town.

At this point, in late 2012, the custodians of this heritage decided to mount a rescue operation. They slipped thousands of documents out by night and transported them by road and boat to Bamako, hundreds of miles to the southwest. They were determined to preserve the memories and the evidence of an ancient, tolerant, and diverse Islamic practice. Their commitment can be followed in an April 25, 2013, article in the *New Republic*, "The Brazen Bibliophiles of Timbuktu: How a Team of Sneaky Librarians Duped Al-Qaeda." It is very much like that of the Senegambian, Ghanaian, and other West African Muslims that we have sought to portray in this project.[18]

---

[18] For background on the disaffection of the Tuareg and Arab Malians, and a profound study of internal racism in West Africa, consult Bruce Hall, *The History of Race in West Africa* (Cambridge University Press, 2011).

# *BOOK REVIEWS*

DOI: 10.5192/215409930501123

Ousman Murzik Kobo. *Unveiling Modernity in Twentieth-Century West African Islamic Reforms*. Leiden: Brill, Islam in Africa Series volume 14, 2012. 384 pp. $186.00.

Ousman Kobo's book is a comparative history of Wahhabi movements in Burkina Faso[1] and Ghana[2] from their origins in the late colonial period through their expansion, decline, and later transformation in the first fifty years of independence. In the footsteps of Lansiné Kaba's pioneering study,[3] the author uses the term "Wahhabism" in a nonreified and neutral sense, against the narrow and derogative inflection given by some local detractors. Kobo refers to Wahhabism to broadly name a new turn in Islamic reform in the decisive context of West Africa's sociopolitical transformations in the mid- to late twentieth century. Going beyond generic conceptualizations, *Unveiling Modernity in Twentieth-Century West African Islamic Reforms* offers thickly descriptive and diachronic analyses of a number of Wahhabi-inclined leaders and organizations in Ouagadougou and Bobo-Dioulasso (with a focus on Mossi society) as well as in Tamale, Kumasi, and Accra. Through these case studies, the book sheds light on West African Wahhabis' plural yet congruous quest for spiritual purity and social reform as they imagined and tried to implement it locally.

Two main themes run through the book. The first emphasizes the local, indigenous origins of Wahhabi reformism in its West African version, contrary to the view that it was a mere translation of contemporary Middle Eastern influences. Wahhabi ideas actually emerged from impassioned local religious contestations over Islamic orthodoxy and specifically Sufi rituals, paving the way for the rise of separate, Sunna-oriented communities.

[1] Haute Volta until 1984.

[2] Gold Coast before 1957.

[3] Lansiné Kaba, *The Wahhabiyya: Islamic Reform and Politics in French West Africa* (Evanston, Ill.: Northwestern University Press, 1974).

*Islamic Africa,* VOL. 5, NO. 1, 2014. ISSN 2154-0993.  www.islamicafricajournal.org

In Burkina Faso from 1963, three Muslim intellectuals—Muhammad Malick Sana, Sayouba Ouédraogo, and later Aboubacar Kanonzoe—were the first to publicly condemn some practices of the local Hamawiyya-Tijaniyya. Kanonzoa explained that they went from being disciples of Sheikh Boubacar Sawodogo to becoming students of the Prophet Muhammad (of note, the book offers a substantial treatment of the little known yet influential figure of Sheikh Sawodogo of the Rahmatoulaye branch of the Hamawiyya, with emphasis on his avoidance approach toward French colonial authorities).

In Ghana, Kobo dates the earliest emergence of Wahhabi-inclined ideas to the early 1950s and the agency of two local (and up to now hardly studied) religious entrepreneurs. In Tamale, then capital of the Northern Territories of the Gold Coast, the scholar Yussif Afajura rejected the *tarbiyya* as un-Islamic. The *tarbiyya* was a Tijani litany said to enable one to see God, introduced into the region after the Senegalese Sheikh Ibrahim Niasse's historic 1952 visit to Ghana. Afajura then consolidated a community of "rejecters" around what became a major madrasa, both known as Ambariyya. In Kumasi, the lead reformist was an original figure: the Asante Adam Appiedu, another major educational entrepreneur of postcolonial Ghanaian Islam. From the 1970s in Burkina as in Ghana, these local reformist leaders and movements moved closer to the Arab-Islamic world and in turn evolved in ways more consubstantial to mainstream Wahhabi dogma and practice.

The book's second main theme is an examination of its Wahhabis' ambivalent engagement *vis-à-vis* modernity. Kobo revisits the scholarly debates on Western, Islamic, and alternative modernities and contributes to the literature by taking the "modernity talk" of West African Wahhabis seriously. He demonstrates that Wahhabis' triple heritage—African, Islamic, and (colonial) European—mingled to create a distinctive modernist style of West African Islamic reform. As Kobo writes: "in spite of cultural differences, the rest is in the West and the West is in the rest . . . This empirically visible human interaction, albeit culturally contingent, cannot be repressed by ideologically-driven notions of cultural impropriety" (xxxiii).

*Unveiling Modernity* emphasizes the fact that in both Burkina Faso and Ghana, secularly educated Muslims, fluent in French or in English, played a decisive role within the first nationwide Wahhabi associations: the 1974 *Mouvement Sunnite de Haute Volta* (later *du Burkina Faso*), and the 1972 Islamic Research and Reformation Center, founded by Hajj Umar Ibrahim in Accra. To a large extent, it was the association of Islamic and secularly trained scholars which made the Wahhabi style of reform attractive to a growing public in West Africa in the 1970s and 1980s, and contributed, beyond Wahhabi circles, to revive Islam and even reform Sufi thought and practice. The dissociation between these two groups that occurred beginning in the 1990s, along with the shrinking of oil money and other factors, led to a relative decline and transformation of Wahhabi revivalism in the region.

The book, a revised version of the author's Ph.D. dissertation, is an original and important study on many counts. It is innovative as a cross-regional comparison between a Francophone country and an Anglophone one. The comparison further straddles the historical periods, from the pre- to the postcolonial ages. Kobo's comparative agenda aptly brings to light what is emic or specific to national domains as well as the fluidity of transnational experiences and influences (though Burkinabe Muslims migrated to Ghana from the early twentieth century, what the book describes are mostly separate though parallel evolutions).

Though voices now call for more geographical diversification, the historiography of Islam in West Africa is only slowly emerging from its longtime focus on Senegal, northern Nigeria, and other Muslim-majority regions. *Unveiling Modernity* fills a gap, as there are too few studies on the Islamic history of Ghana and Burkina Faso (for the latter country, especially in English). The book unveils many unknown or little-known Islamic scholars, communities, and initiatives: it is an indispensable source of new data.

Beyond the Wahhabi focus and its empirical wealth, the book is a broader investigation of Islamic revivals and declines that is inclusive of Sufi input in Islamic reformation past and present, as well as an analysis of Islam's capacity to "domesticate" external historical contingencies. The book is exemplary for the transparency of its methodology and its pedagogical ambitions.

Kobo witnessed some Tijani-Wahhabi disputes in Ghana as a curious and devout child, and embarked as an adult thirty years later to conduct research on both Ghana and Burkina Faso. As explained in the book's preface, *Unveiling Modernity* is also a personal reflection on history. Such intimate-cum-intellectual insights are rarely found in history books of the kind. They are genuine in their concern to delineate the researcher's "positionality" *vis-à-vis* the very questions that led him from childhood curiosity to academic research, from local to global knowledge, to craft a praiseworthy piece of scholarship.

*Marie Miran-Guyon, École des Hautes Études en Sciences Sociales (EHESS, France); associated in 2013–15 to the Institut de Recherche pour le Développement (IRD, France and Côte d'Ivoire) and the Université Alassane Ouattara (Côte d'Ivoire)*

Stig Jarle Hansen. *Al-Shabaab in Somalia: The History and Ideology of a Militant Islamist Group, 2005–2012.* New York: Oxford University Press, 2012. 195 pp.; chronology, glossary, bibliography, index. $37.50.

Stig Jarle Hansen is to be lauded as an expert on Somalia who gets beyond the echo chambers of conferences and the agendas of websites, wading instead into the real world of Somali society and the critical role that Al-Shabaab plays in it. The product of his hard work provides the reader with a superb analysis of Al-Shabaab's ideological and operational mainsprings and the effect that this organization has had on Somalia and the region.

The author paints a picture of an armed group that at once is remarkably successful at the same time that it falls prey to repeated failures. The detailed description of how Al-Shabaab actually governed in areas that it controlled by 2009 provides concrete details about what kinds and how much taxation sustained the organization, the services and security that it offered communities, and its mechanisms for ensuring the control and discipline of members and the wider society. In this respect, Al-Shabaab emerged as the most coherent, well-organized, and extensive administration that southern Somalia had known in the past two decades. Hansen repeatedly notes the ways in which the organization's record of governance was superior to that of the several internationally sponsored authorities.

At the same time, Hansen paints a picture of fragmentation and contention. In numerous examples, Al-Shabaab confronts clan politics through a conscious strategy of incorporating clan leaders who also share ideological and personal connections to Al-Shabaab's leaders. This enabled the organization to direct the strengths of clan loyalties for easy victories. But his practice also imported clan conflicts that, once embedded, also could fragment the organization.

These two pictures remain in tension with one another throughout the book and raise broader questions for the reader about the nature of Islamic thought and political action in the Somali context. Most scholars appear to believe that identity is socially constructed. Therefore, if Al-Shabaab really could organize society so effectively in areas that it controlled, one would imagine that the idea of clan-based politics—an idea already widely blamed for many of Somalia's woes—would be vulnerable. What then explains the resilience of the clan logic? One might imagine that Somalia should be especially hospitable to an Islamist internationalist message, given the successes of Al-Shabaab governance and the appeal as an alternative to the old status quo. Hansen indeed shows the durability of an Islamist internationalism among key Al-Shabaab leaders; but again, with a relatively limited effect on the overall tempo of politics.

In a sense, this book about the successes of Al-Shabaab is also a book about its failures. The dedicated Al-Qaeda-inspired internationalists succeed in attracting supporters but fail to overcome the instrumental calculations of the local political figures that they must absorb into their organization if they are to fight and govern effectively. In old-fashioned terms, Al-Shabaab never succeeds in mobilizing the masses directly. Their "liberated zone" still depends upon deals with local intermediaries who provide ultimate protection and can tap the loyalties of members of their communities.

These challenges facing Al-Shabaab's internationalists raise questions about the capacity of this brand of Islamic thought to shape a society's grand narratives in ways that challenge the parochialisms of Somali politics and society. As Hansen notes in his conclusion, this weakness is not unique to Al-Shabaab. All revolutionary groups struggle to sort out issues of governance and to manage existing local authority structures. But perhaps Somali politics presents special challenges to broad ideological agendas that may be related to the consequences of the collapse of centralized state authority and the proliferation of multiple armed groups. Thus those who wonder about the fates of Islamist internationalists in other places where central state authority has collapsed will benefit from reading Hansen's excellent book.

This book, filled as it is with exquisite detail, stimulates thinking about these bigger questions and thus is much more successful than the typical specialist volume. The specialist will be particularly pleased; the encyclopedic details about individuals, where they are from, who they know, and what they have done is like gold. In this regard, the only wish of this reader was that Hansen had provided a few more details about how the research for this book was carried out, about how one visits Mogadishu in difficult times, and how one evaluates the credibility of information that one receives. This is but a quibble about a book that clearly sets the standard for scholarship on the subject of Al-Shabaab and its influence on political thought and action inside and outside Somalia.

*William Reno, Northwestern University*

Valerie J. Hoffman. *The Essentials of Ibadi Islam*. Syracuse: Syracuse University Press, 2011. 328 pp. $39.95.

*The Essentials of Ibadi Islam* is a long-overdue overview of one of the most understudied and misunderstood sects in Islam. Having emerged in the early Islamic period, Ibadism, a sect that is neither Sunni nor Shiʾi, is influential today mainly in North Africa and Oman and is rich not only in history, but also in theology, philosophy, and jurisprudence. Although several works on Ibadism do exist in the English language—most notably Adam R. Gaiser's *Muslims, Scholars, Soldiers: The Origin and Elaboration of the Ibadi Imamate Traditions*—none of them explains Ibadi theology. Valerie J. Hoffman, whose volume is the first book-length work on the theology of modern Ibadism in English, has done a superb job in introducing Ibadi literature—a literature that "is often very long, dry, dense, and difficult to understand" (5)—to Western audiences.

*The Essentials of Ibadi Islam* is divided into three parts: the first part is a long and detailed introduction of Ibadi history as well as of the role of Ibadism in the development of Islamic thought. Parts 2 and 3 provide annotated translations of two complementary modern Ibadi theological texts. In the introduction, the author discusses the origin and political history of the Ibadiyya, the development of Ibadism as a distinct sect of Islam, and the distinctive teachings of Ibadi Islam. In the introduction's section on the political history of Ibadism, Hoffman lays out the Ibadi perspective on the early Caliphate and how this perspective differs from that of the Sunnis and the Shiʾa.

The author then moves to discuss how the Ibadis identify with much of the Kharijite history, which is evident in a theological primer entitled *Al-ʿAqida ʾl-Wahbiyya*, or *The Wahbi Creed*. Hoffman presents Ibadism as a moderate Khariji sect that emerged under the leadership of ʿAbdallah b. Ibad (or Abad) who broke with the more violent and extreme Kharijites. This section concludes with a discussion of the emergence of the first Ibadi state in the eighth century in the Hadramawt region, the establishment of the Ibadi imamate in North Africa, and the role of Ibadism in the political history of modern Oman.

In the next section of the introduction, Hoffman provides the reader with a list of Ibadi theological, legal, historical, and poetical works written between the eighth and twentieth centuries. This section serves as a great reference for those interested in early and modern Ibadi literature. The following is a list of the topics discussed: the status of sinning Muslims;

religious affiliation (*walaya*) and dissociation (*baraʾa*); reward and punishment in the afterlife; free will and predestination; the anthropomorphic descriptions of God; reason and revelation; the unity of God, his essence, and attributes; the creation of the Qurʾan; and jurisprudence. This section by itself is a great contribution to the field of theological studies and is quite useful for those interested in Islamic theology.

In part 2, Hoffman provides an annotated translation of *Al-ʿAqida ʾl-Wahbiyya* (*The Wahbiyya Doctrine*) by Nasir b. Salim b. ʿUdayyam al-Rawahi (d. 1920). This primer in Ibadi doctrine is divided into seven chapters with an introduction by the author. Al-Rawahi's primer covers many different Islamic theological schools as well as differences between the Ibadis of North Africa, Oman, and Zanzibar. In this text, al-Rawahi offers a brief introduction to Ibadi doctrine as well as a thorough discussion of many different Muslim groups, past and present. Some of the theological issues that interested the Ibadis and are discussed in the primer are God's unity, essence, and attributes and the creation or eternity of the Qurʾan. Hoffman notes that the Ibadis retain an interest in these topics as a way to "defend doctrines that set them apart from other Muslims" (48). The primer is written in the form of a student's questions and the teacher's answers.

The theological primer contains lessons ranging in topics from the science in theology and the definition of *tawhid* (God's oneness) to the most important religious obligation, the three statements of faith, and the knowledge of God's oneness through the intellect. Also discussed are lessons pertaining to the roots of knowledge of God's oneness, the attributes of God, and the origin of the word of the name of majesty (Allah).

The primer also deals with interesting topics such as God's attributes of essence and of acts, the roots of religion, the impossibility of seeing God, the types and regulations of religious affiliation (*walaya*) and dissociation (*baraʾa*), the six religions and the regulations concerning people who are not of Muhammad's community (*umma*), the meaning of the *jizya* (protection tax on non-Muslims), its requirement, the goal behind the *jizya*, and the limits on a Muslim ruler in collecting the *jizya*. This section on the *jizya* from an Ibadi perspective is helpful for Muslim theologians who are interested in exploring further the meaning and goal of this Qurʾanic injunction.

Part 3 of Hoffman's work is an annotated translation of the seventh section of chapter 3 and the entirety of chapter 4 of part 3 of *Kitab Maʿalim al-Din* (*The Characteristics of Religion*) by ʿAbd al-ʿAziz al-Thamini al-Musʾabi (d. 1808). The translated selection of the book deals with matters pertaining to God's power and human acts.

*The Essentials of Ibadi Islam* is important and essential reading for students in Islamic studies departments and programs as well as specialists in Islamic theology. What makes this work useful, informative, and interesting is the way the chapters weave Ibadi theology with the theology of other Muslim groups such as the Kharijites, the Muʾtazila, the Ashʾarites, the Maturidites, the Shiʾa, and other Ibadis of different regions. This juxtaposition of the theologies of different Islamic theological schools makes this work a great reference book on Islamic theology.

Not only does Hoffman make available to Western audiences a wealth of literature on Ibadi Islam and Ibadi theology but she has also managed to present Ibadism in a fair and balanced way. *The Essentials of Ibadi Islam* does correct some of the misperceptions about the sect and challenges Muslim and non-Muslim scholars of Islam to rethink their views of Ibadism. This book is of real importance as it contributes an essential literature to the fields of religious and Middle Eastern studies while also filling a gap in the field of Islamic studies. Not only does Hoffman present us with the challenge to investigate further Ibadi history, theology, and jurisprudence but she has also set the path for us to begin the journey into a world yet to be discovered.

*Hussam S. Timani, Christopher Newport University*